How
to trace
your military
ancestors
in Australia and New Zealand

R. H. Montague

Hale & Iremonger

By the same author
*Dress and Insignia of the British Army in Australia
and New Zealand 1770 to 1870*

Typeset, printed & bound by
Southwood Press Pty Limited
80–92 Chapel Street, Marrickville, NSW

For the publisher
Hale & Iremonger Pty Limited
GPO Box 2552, Sydney, NSW

*National Library of Australia Cataloguing-in-publication
entry*
Montague, R. H. (Ronald H.)
   How to trace your military ancestors.

   Bibliography.
   Includes index.
   ISBN 0 86806 340 1 (casebound)
   ISBN 0 86806 341 X (paperbound)

   1. Soldiers — Australia — Genealogy —
   Handbooks, manuals, etc. 2. Soldiers — New
   Zealand — Genealogy — Handbooks, manuals,
   etc. 3. Australia — Genealogy — Handbooks,
   manuals, etc. 4. New Zealand — Genealogy —
   Handbooks, manuals, etc. I. Title.

929'.1'07209

Contents

Illustrations

Acknowledgements

The illustrations on pp. 2, 10 and 44 are from paintings by R. J. Marrion. The photograph on p. 80 is published by permission of the State Library of NSW, that on p. 116 is reproduced by permission of the Newcastle Region Public Library, the maps on pp. 56 and 57 by permission of the Archives Office of NSW, the Pay and Muster Roll (WO 12/5266) on p. 30 is reproduced by permission of the Public Record Office, Kew, England.

PART ONE

General introduction — the phases of military history in Australia and New Zealand — reasons for the presence of British troops — administration and organisation of the British Army — historical background — why the records are so complex — the Public Record Office in London — the War Office holdings — those which are biographical and genealogical significance — a comprehensive list of officers' and soldiers' documents — records of pensioners and widows — East India Company Records

Captain, NSW Corps, c.1805

General introduction

The phases of military history in Australia and New Zealand

A family historian tracing a military ancestor encounters a system of record-keeping which differs considerably from records kept by any civilian agency. Many Army books and documents were meticulously kept and conscientiously preserved but inevitably some are missing. Just how complete an officer's or soldier's documents will be, must depend upon the period in which he served.

Broadly speaking the military histories of Australia and New Zealand can be divided into three:

1   *The Imperial* began in Australia with the arrival of the First Fleet in 1788 and in New Zealand with the appointment of a British Resident, Captain William Hobson, in 1840. In both colonies British garrison force was established.

2   *The Colonial* the period when colonial governments formed part-time and regular armed forces.

3   *The Commonwealth and Dominion period* began in Australia when the Commonwealth Government took over control of all armed forces. In New Zealand this process had begun when the control of local armed forces was transferred from provincial to central government control in 1876.

The Imperial phase began with the arrival of four companies of Marines (not yet Royal), in 1788. This force of about 200 men was intended to serve as a defence against possible attack by the French or hostile natives. It was also expected to preserve some vestige of law and order among the convict and government population. Several Marine Officers were ordered to administer civil as well as military justice by serving as magistrates while most of the Non-Commissioned Officers (NCOs) and private Marines were detailed off to guard the convicts and to police the settlement. All ranks found their non-military duties distasteful and many objected openly. Soon after the establishment of the Sydney Cove settlement, Governor Phillip approached the Marines and suggested that they might wish to settle in the colony permanently. Offers of free land attracted little enthusiasm as conditions were bad, food was scarce, clothing was in short supply, and the building of any kind of shelter was very slow.

However, by the time the first batch of New South Wales Corps men arrived at Sydney to relieve the Marines, conditions had become a little better. When volunteers were called for on this occasion, a number of Marines chose to settle on land grants in New South Wales and on Norfolk Island. There were also a number of men who wished to continue in the Army and this option attracted a cash bounty of three guineas (£3.3s.) which was more than four months' pay for a Marine Private. An extra company was added to the New South Wales Corps, formed from Marines re-engaged in the Army for further service. A Marine officer, Captain George Johnston, also transferred to command the new company and seventeen years later achieved some notoriety during the overthrow of Governor William Bligh.

Captain Bligh RN, took office as the Governor of New South Wales in August 1806 and almost immediately friction developed between himself and the military officers. A traditional Royal Navy man, he strongly disapproved of officers being involved in trade. He especially deplored the use of liquor as a form of currency which later gave the New South Wales Corps the nickname of 'Rum Corps'.

Most of the Army officers and many civilian traders and landholders were resolved to get rid of Bligh. Matters appeared to come to a head when a legal battle ensued between the Governor and George Johnston, then a major. On 26 January 1808 he led a party of soldiers to Government House, arrested Governor Bligh and took over the duties of Government himself. Johnston remained in charge until Macquarie arrived in 1810, when Bligh was re-appointed for a nominal twenty-four hours and Johnston returned to England to stand trial by court-martial. Johnston was subsequently cashiered (a mild sentence) and was able to return to New South Wales as a civilian.

During the nineteen years that the New South Wales Corps was in

New South Wales many of its officers and rank and file were discharged from the Army to settle either in Van Diemen's Land or New South Wales. Many were granted extensive areas of land, handed out on a more liberal scale when there was no governor in office and the administration was entirely in the hands of the military. This procedure was curbed while Governor Bligh was in office.

Bligh's successor, Lachlan Macquarie, did not condone officers or soldiers quitting the Army to become settlers but he was always sympathetic to old soldiers who had served out their time. During his term of office many of the veterans who were permitted to settle became prominent citizens.

From the time that the New South Wales Corps (re-designated as the 102nd Regiment) left Australia, a succession of twenty-four in-fantry regiments came and went. One regiment, the 65th, served for almost twenty years, another, the 77th, remained for about seven months. The average stay in the colonies was about five years. In addition to the infantry there were batteries and companies of Royal Artillery and Royal Engineers. The former were responsible for the defence of the coastline and the latter constructed a great number of bridges, roads and public buildings. It was an officer of the Royal Engineers, Colonel Barney, who designed Circular Quay in Sydney while his colleague, Captain Martindale, contributed much to the New South Wales railway system.

To the twenty-four regiments and two support corps should be added companies of Staff Corps and Veterans and in New Zealand the troops had the benefits of Hospital, Commissariat, and Transport Companies. These are of particular significance to the genealogist because most of them settled permanently in Australia. Without the assistance of computerised technology it would be very difficult to estimate just how many of the Imperial troops remained. Taking into account those who served with the Marines and New South Wales Corps and the smaller numbers who were in the Artillery, Engineers and Staff Corps, it might be suggested that around 5,000 or so could have stayed. This figure would not include the 627 men who deserted from the Army in Australia and New Zealand between the years 1800 and 1870. Men who deserted during the earlier period would have had little chance of survival in the bush but during the 1840 to 1870 period deserters usually found no difficulty in finding work and becoming absorbed into the local population. The greater proportion of these were married or were soon married on returning to civil life; most had large families.

Some genealogical studies have shown that these military immigrants have produced a prodigious number of descendants. Research up to 1986 on the family of Sergeant Thomas Clark of the 28th Regiment, found a total of 3,683 descendants through six generations. Families of twelve or more occurred frequently during the 19th and early 20th centuries.

The first British troops to spend any time in New Zealand were members of the 57th (West Middlesex) Regiment who were guarding a party of convicts bound for Norfolk Island. The convicts mutinied, overpowered the guards and took charge of the ship and when the water supply was low the convicts compelled the crew to put in at a New Zealand whaling port. The troops went ashore, the whaling ships surrounded the mutineers' vessel and captured the convicts who were subsequently hanged. The sergeant in charge of the troops was reduced to the ranks for inefficiency. This happened in 1830 and it was almost ten years before a small detachment of the 80th (Staffordshire) Regiment landed near to Auckland to be present at the signing of the Treaty of Waitangi. These men did not take part in the first Maori war.

The first European defence force in New Zealand consisted of companies of the 96th and 99th (Lanarkshire) Regiments both of which had been stationed in Australia. From 1840 until the withdrawal of British troops in 1870 there were eleven infantry regiments and six support corps stationed in New Zealand; mainly in the North Island. The 14th and 43rd Regiments were serving in the India stations (Bombay, Calcutta, or Madras) before moving to the Australasian region; the 50th and 77th came fresh from the war in the Crimea.

On a per capita basis it would appear that the majority of the British troops showed interest in settling in a new country. From 1843 most were serving a ten-year engagement as opposed to the old system of signing for 'unlimited service' (that is for life). 'Life' in the Army had become healthier as medical services improved and the climate in New Zealand compared more favourably with that of the British Isles than most of the military stations of the time. Many British officers and soldiers either transferred into, or joined the local militia forces and became absorbed into the fast-growing European population of New Zealand.

A high proportion of the British soldiers who settled in Australia served as Mounted Police. Officers and rank and file were seconded for this duty from around 1823 until civilian police forces were established during the 1850s and 1860s. The practice began at a time when bushrangers were on the increase in New South Wales and attacks on European settlers by Aborigines in Van Diemen's Land were becoming more organised as European settlement encroached on tribal lands.

Commanding officers of the regiments disliked the system of transfers to the Mounted Police as it meant the loss of some of their best men, usually permanently. Soldiers would transfer to incoming regiments when their former regiment left the colony. For the officers this service offered few advantages. After 1830 the amount of the pay they received from the colonial government was deducted from their Army pay but for the NCOs and Privates it did offer a better life: freedom from the harsh discipline of Army supervision, free rations and a more comfortable uniform which was based on that worn by the 14th Light Dragoons. By 1834 there was a small detachment of the 4th (King's Own) Regiment on duty as Mounted Police in the Port Phillip settlement which was to become the Colony of Victoria. In New South Wales the Mounted Police was organised into four divisions which were manned by officers and rank and file from the 4th and 17th Regiments. The Headquarter Division was located at Sydney and included Parramatta, Windsor, Liverpool, and Campbelltown. The 1st Division was stationed at Bathurst, the 2nd at Goulburn Plains, and the 3rd at Jerry's Plains on the Hunter River. The total strength of the New South Wales Mounted Police was at this time seven officers and about 107 NCOs and Privates. As time passed these numbers were to increase considerably.

During the goldrush era of the 1850s in Victoria a number of officers joined the Gold Commission and many of the rank and file served as gold escorts. It was during this period that civilian police forces were formed and while the New South Wales Force continued to recruit Army men many who joined the Victorian force were former convicts from Tasmania. Some authorities believed that this tended to give the force an unsavoury reputation during the time of the Eureka Stockade in 1854. In other colonies preference seemed to be given to ex-Army men. From the mid-1820s the Pay and Muster Rolls (WO 12) show the officers and rank and file who were detailed off for duty in the Mounted Police; this continued until the civil authorities took over responsibility for police organisation. In New South Wales during the early 1850s the term 'Road Patrol' was used instead of Mounted Police.

At the present time State police forces still hold some of their early records which include personal details about their military pioneers. Inquiries about early police records should be addressed to the force's Public Relations Officer.

The second phase dealing with locally raised armed forces began early in Australia's colonial history with a small, short-lived militia raised on Norfolk Island in 1788. Two companies, known as Loyal Associations, were formed in Sydney and Parramatta. Governor King authorised these during the latter part of 1800 because of anticipated unrest among some Irish convicts and a French invasion of the colony was feared. Members of the Loyal Associations wore the uniform of the New South Wales Corps, met for drill and musket practice every Saturday afternoon, and took part in quelling the Castle Hill uprising in March 1804. Following this nine men were hanged, a number shot, and others flogged. The companies were disbanded in 1810 (with regret in some quarters) when it was believed that the military establishment of Australia was up to strength.

In 1840 Governor Gawler formed a Royal Brigade of Volunteer Militia but this too was short-lived. Nothing further was done about any local armed forces until 1854 when it was thought that Russia might invade the settled areas on the Australian coast using India as a jumping-off point. Some half-hearted efforts were made towards raising a Volunteer Force; New South Wales formed a troop of cavalry, six small companies of infantry, and two batteries of artillery. A part-time force, its members were unpaid, supplying their own uniforms, equipment, and horses. The Government magnanimously provided rifles, swords, and ammunition although Queen Victoria graciously met the cost of 100 rifles out of her own purse.

After the Crimean War of 1854 to 1856 peace was made with Russia and interest in volunteer armed forces waned, the small amount of government assistance was withdrawn but a few members continued to meet unofficially. In 1861 there was another war scare closer to the Australasian colonies. France was expanding its empire in the South Pacific, Russia had built a naval base in Vladivostok, rebel Maoris were active again in New Zealand, and North America was on the verge of civil war. The colonial governments were spurred into action and a more serious attempt was made to form a local volunteer military force with adequate government assistance. Almost every town and settlement of any size raised troops of cavalry, batteries of Artillery or companies of infantry; the larger coastal towns formed batteries of garrison artillery. A high proportion of the male population in Australia came forward to offer their services; and in

New Zealand the need for armed forces was an accepted fact of life for all males between sixteen and sixty years of age.

Australian Volunteers were still unpaid although all items of equipment and clothing were provided. They were promised that in the event of the Force being called out for full-time duty all ranks would be paid at a liberal rate. This promise was kept in July 1861 when miners threatened violence at Lambing Flat; the volunteer infantry in Sydney were detailed for duties which had been carried out by the 12th British Regiment.

During the 1860s the anti-Imperial Liberal Government in Britain sought to withdraw its country's troops from all the major colonies; these included Canada, Australia, and New Zealand. Britain still provided naval protection but the self-governing colonies were asked that their military forces become 'self-reliant'. The last of the Regular British Army left New Zealand early in 1870 and by September of the same year the last of the British Artillery, Engineers, and Infantry in Australia had sailed for England.

The European population of New Zealand was still embroiled in the final stages of the Maori uprisings; the six Australian colonies had volunteer military forces and very small regular forces, all in varying degrees of efficiency. They were now faced with the prospect of establishing small permanent armies.

By 1880 Australia could raise only 9,000 men which included permanent, militia, and unpaid volunteers from a population close to 2,000,000. It had been difficult to maintain interest in the Volunteer Force and some colonial governments offered grants of fifty acres (20.3 ha.) to men who were certified as efficient for five consecutive years. Although many took advantage of the scheme few actually worked the land but usually sold it to speculators. Fortunately for the family historian the land grant scheme created a lot of documentation and much of this is still available in Parliamentary Papers (*Votes & Proceedings*), and in all Australian State Archives offices.

From the 1880s to 1900 interest in matters military lessened during periods of world peace and was stimulated when any threat arose. March 1885 saw the first contingent of Australian soldiers sail away to fight in an overseas war. A battalion of infantry, a section of Medical Corps were manned from the Volunteer Force and a battery of field artillery was constituted from the Permanent Artillery of New South Wales to serve in the Sudan war. Although Queensland and Victoria offered to send troops to the Sudan the New South Wales contingent was sufficiently prepared to be able to land in the Sudan port of

Suakin within twenty-eight days. Many of the Australian military records of this period have been lost but some of the documentation generated at the time of the Sudan war has been preserved at the Australian War Memorial and the New South Wales State Archives Office.

By the time the Australian Federal Constitution passed the responsibility for defence to the Commonwealth in 1901, the armed forces of the six former colonies had increased to a total of 29,000 men. The more populous States of New South Wales, Victoria, and Queensland contributed more than 20,000 of these. At this time Australia and New Zealand were involved in the South African War and were training and dispatching troops and transporting materials to the theatre of war. At Federation there were more than 3,000,000 people in Australia.

The years between the South African War and World War I saw many changes in Army organisation throughout the old British Empire. In Australia many of the old intercolonial rivalries remained to hinder the integration of the six former armed forces into one unified Commonwealth Military Force. In 1908 both Australian and New Zealand governments passed a Defence Bill. The Australian Act made it compulsory for school boys between the ages of twelve and eighteen to undergo military training. A year later the New Zealand Act brought in a system of compulsory military training with the newly constituted Territorial Force. In 1911 Australia introduced compulsory military training, on a part-time basis, for adult males up to the age of twenty-six. The Force formed by this system was known at different times as the Citizen Force and the Militia. During World War I the Australian Imperial Force remained voluntary; two attempts by the Federal Government to introduce a universal conscription system failed. The form of training which had been introduced in 1911 continued until 1929. New Zealand introduced conscription ballots during 1916 under the Military Service Act; this was organised by recruiting districts and those who were called up were notified in the *New Zealand Gazette*.

Records of individuals who served with the Second Australian or New Zealand Expeditionary Forces are well preserved. In addition to the official personal documents there are war diaries, Medal Rolls, personal files, and casualty lists kept at the Australian War Memorial, Canberra, ACT, and equivalent institutions in New Zealand. The involvement of both countries in postwar conflicts such as the

Malayan Emergency, Korea, and Vietnam has created yet another set of records of military ancestors.

Administration and organisation of the British Army

Historical background

Before the English Civil War of 1642 to 1649 there was no standing Army; part-time or militia forces were raised in times of war and were disbanded when the emergency had passed.

Oliver Cromwell formed his 'New Model Army' in 1645 and this was the first time that England had an Army that was uniformly clothed, fed, and paid with some kind of centralised control.

After the restoration of Charles II to the throne in 1660 the nucleus of the Regular Army was formed from the remains of the two warring factions; a regiment of cavalry and foot soldiers was taken from the Parliamentary (Roundhead) Army and the same from the Royalist (Cavalier) Army who had joined King Charles II during his period of exile. These four regiments were intended to serve as a royal body-guard and to add a little pomp and pageantry to State occasions. The Regular Army was established between 1660 and 1680 and became a part of an overseas defence force sent to guard Britain's newly acquired colonies such as Jamaica and Tangiers. Following the deposition of King James II (VII of Scotland), the 'Glorious Revolution' of 1688 established a Bill of Rights which made it illegal for the country to keep a standing Army in times of peace.

Such an Army would only be acceptable to Parliament if its command were fragmented and its organisation divided between a number of government offices and agencies. This is still reflected in the character and locations of Army Records.

When the Act of Union amalgamated the English and Scottish Parliaments in 1707 Scotland contributed to the expansion of the Regular Army of Britain. By 1748 it had grown to a total of twenty-five regiments of cavalry and sixty-six of infantry; three of the cavalry regiments were Horse Guards and three of the infantry were Foot Guards. Of the sixty-six regiments of infantry ten were Marines (not yet 'Royal'), three were Fuziliers (Fusiliers), who were specially trained to guard the quasi-civilian artillery, seven had been granted 'Royal' titles, three were Highlanders and one was raised for service in North America. The rest were given numerical titles in order of seniority but were usually known by the names of the colonels who raised and commanded them.

The strength of the battalion or regiment has varied from time to time. In 1645 Cromwell led regiments that were as much as 1,200 strong but as the number of musketeers increased they were reduced to a more manageable size. By 1700 they were around 450 men of all ranks but when the two flank companies were added to a regiment its total strength was usually around 600 to 800 men. Before 1862 there are frequent references to 'Grenadier' and 'Light' companies. The Grenadiers were the tallest men of the regiment who were trained to throw grenades and usually led an assault; the Light were the shorter, faster moving men who were trained for skirmishing and scouting. It was found to be undesirable that most of the more highly trained men were concentrated in two companies and the plan was discontinued by 1862. The value of light company men had been noted many years before and several Light Infantry Regiments had been formed to carry out the same duties.

The companies were commanded by Captains who were sometimes responsible for raising them. Captains paid from £3,000 to £4,000 for commissions, and hoped to run their own companies like businesses, showing profits. Each Captain was usually assisted by two or three Lieutenants and perhaps one or two newly commissioned Ensigns (or Cornets for Cavalry) who were, most likely, still of school-age. Until early in the 19th century there was little formal training for young officers except for those entering the Artillery or Engineers. As Ensigns were required to carry the regimental colours in battle and because so many died, the rank of Colour Sergeant was created in 1813.

In addition to officers each company had an establishment of NCOs. Usually it was three Sergeants, three Corporals, and two Drummers who could also be either Buglers or Trumpeters. The latter were usually boys between fourteen and eighteen-years-old. Each regiment had a Paymaster, a Quartermaster, a Surgeon, an Assistant Surgeon and an Adjutant. These were referred to as Staff Officers and in later years might include a Chaplain. The Adjutant was assisted by a Sergeant-Major who was the most senior NCO of the Regiment; the title Warrant-Officer was not used until 1881.

During times of war new regiments were raised and after the war were either disbanded, reduced or re-numbered. This has created some confusion for both military and family historians.

In 1783 the majority of infantry regiments were given either county or district titles in addition to their numbers. This system was discontinued in 1881 when the last of the Cardwell reforms amalgamated pairs of regiments into 1st and 2nd battalions with the exception of the

1st to the 25th Regiments of Foot because they were already formed into two battalions. By the end of the Napoleonic wars the British Army had grown to about 250,000 men but after a period of large-scale demobilisation the Army stagnated. Public apathy and false government economies led to an almost continuous process of reduction in total strength of armed forces. Only a nucleus of Front Line units were maintained but always at the expense of supporting services.

The Army was being called on to garrison the ever-increasing number of colonial settlements, many of which were in remote parts of the world. In such places soldiers would be exposed to the extremes of climate, dangerous environment, and the most primitive of living conditions.

During the early stages of the Crimean War many of these factors were presented to the British public for the first time by the London *Times* journalist, William Howard Russell. General indignation followed his reports and brought about the establishment of new boards, commissions and committees ordered to investigate Army departments responsible for the deficiencies. Mainly these departments were those concerned with transport, clothing, feeding, and medical attention.

Before the Crimean War ended in 1856 many of the investigative boards' recommendations were being effected. More lasting benefits came from reforms in matters of administration and organisation which continued for almost twenty years. This did much to end complexities arising from the multiplicity of offices that claimed some jurisdiction over Army affairs.

Although the Regular Army had been formed in 1660 the head of its organisation was not made a political appointment until 1704 but as Secretary *at* War the appointee was not made responsible to Parliament until 1783. Ten years later the post of Commander-in-Chief was re-introduced and the following year a Secretary of State *for* War was appointed. This office became, in theory at least, answerable to Parliament but the actual jurisdiction over matters of Army policy was shared between the politically independent Secretary *at* War and the Commander-in-Chief. The Commander-in-Chief was personally responsible for raising armed forces when and wherever they were needed but the precise areas of power were never clearly defined.

In 1801 the Offices of Secretary of State *for* War and Secretary of State for the Colonies were combined. At this point the Army became increasingly involved in colonial affairs until the two Offices were separated in 1854. There was a continual power struggle between the Secretary *at* War and the Commander-in-Chief.

Although the Secretary *at* War was responsible for all aspects of Army finance neither he nor the Commander-in-Chief had any authority over the provision of barracks, fortifications or weapons; these came within the purview of the ancient Office known as the Master of Ordnance which governed all matters of discipline and finance for the Artillery and Engineers. The basic food rations for the troops was the responsibility of the Commissariat, a branch of the Treasury. A corps for administering this department was raised in the mid-19th century which, after many changes in title and organisation, became the Army Service Corps in 1888.

Before 1855 there was no rank and file corps to care for the sick and wounded. Regimental surgeons were Staff Officers of the corps to which they were attached. The Army Medical Department, which was entirely administrative, was responsible for the supply of hospitals and surgeons, and issuing medical stores. All matters of discipline came under the control of the Commander-in-Chief.

The condition, design, and provision of soldiers' uniforms were supervised by the Board of General Officers. Court-martials were administered by the Judge-Advocate General and he continued in this position for many years with only a few changes.

From 1855 the following changes were made to administration and organisation of Army affairs. The Offices of War and Colonial Affairs were separated into two departments. The Offices of Secretary at War and for War were amalgamated and the title of War Office was officially adopted in 1857. At the same time the Board of Ordnance was abolished thereby bringing the Artillery and Engineers under the direct control of the War Office. In 1863 the position of Secretary at War was completely abolished and eventually the War Office Act of 1870 brought all branches of Army administration under War Office control.

A further complication in locating Army Records was created by the Honorable East India Company. This once powerful organisation was formed in the early 17th century to foster mercantile interests in India and countries adjacent. To defend its interests the Company formed an Army from locally recruited volunteers which was commanded by British officers who had been training at the HEIC Training College in England. The Indian Mutiny (1857) exposed many weaknesses in the East India Company's methods and in 1858 it was taken over by the British Government. A number of the Company's regiments were then absorbed by the British Army including both cavalry and infantry. These appear in the Army List for 1860.

Location of East India Company records

The India Office Library in London holds a wealth of biographical information on the Armies of the East India Company, from 1600 to 1947, the year of Indian Independence. The collection includes extensive runs of Army Lists and personal details of officers who held the highest positions in the Indian administration down to the most junior private soldier.

The India Office Library has 34,000 volumes and files which deal with the personnel of all branches of the service with a further 10,000 volumes about military affairs. This Library is now a part of the British Library which was formerly known as the British Museum Library.

Locations of Militia records

Occasionally an ancestor may appear in a picture wearing military uniform or be mentioned as serving with the Militia. If the picture were taken before 1907 any records would be held either by the Home Office or at a County Records Office.

In peacetime since Tudor times the Militia came under the jurisdiction of the counties and the ballot for service was held by the parish which was the basic unit of local government. Officers were appointed by the Lords Lieutenant of the counties and came under the control of the Commander-in-Chief in times of war. Militia records from the 18th to the mid-19th centuries are at the Home Office in the class HO/50 and HO/51. County Record Offices usually have a wealth of information on the Militia from the earliest times. They also keep Honour Rolls of the various wars.

The term 'Militia' was applied to the first groups of conscripts in the UK during 1939 and 1940; these were administered entirely by the War Office and the term fell into disuse as the war progressed.

The Public Record Office (PRO) Kew, near London

Officer's records
Officers who served during the Civil War and during the Commonwealth period of 1649 to 1659, both Cavaliers and Roundheads, are listed in Edward Peacock *Army List of Roundheads and*

Cavaliers London, 1863 and the second edition, which was published in 1874, includes an index.

Some parliamentary Army records may be found in the State Papers, *Calendar of State Papers* HMSO, 1875–1886, and these include indexes.

Officer's records which give some personal information may be found on his document of commission, those which refer to his promotion, his resignation or when he was placed on half pay. There were no systematic records of an officer's service kept until the early part of the 19th century.

When beginning biographical research on a Regular Army officer reference to an Army List can prove useful. It will give, at least, the date the commission was granted in both the Army and the Regiment. Manuscript lists were kept from 1702 until 1752 and these are held at the PRO Kew in class WO 64.

Officers who served before 1727 may be traced in Charles Dalton's book, *English Army Lists and Commission Registers*, which was published in London between 1892 and 1904 (6 vols) and also *George I's Army 1714-1727*, London, 1910 and 1912 (2 vols). The first official Army List was published in 1740 and since 1754 these have been published regularly and may be found in many of the larger reference libraries.

Complete sets of Annual Lists from 1754 to 1879 and Quarterly Lists from 1879 to 1900 are kept at the PRO Kew and may be seen in the Reference Room. Monthly lists were published between 1798 and 1940 but from July 1940 the list was given a security classification and was not published. The lists indexed from 1867 include officers of colonial, militia, and territorial units.

Quarterly Army Lists were produced from 1879 until 1922 giving additional information useful to the researcher. These lists include an order of seniority, dates of birth, and promotions. From April 1881 the lists include some details of officers' war service.

From February 1923 until 1950 Half Yearly Lists were produced to replace the Quarterly Lists and these also include a gradation list and also, in the January edition only, a list of retired officers. Both the Half Yearly and Quarterly Lists are restricted publications.

Changes in the format of Army Lists took place in 1968 and in 1971; the Reference Desk at the PRO is able to supply details on request.

In addition to the official Army List a useful unofficial list was compiled by Lieutenant-General H. G. Hart from 1839 and this was continued until 1915. It was produced annually and quarterly and from April 1881 includes details of the officer's war service which is not available from any other source. Copies of Hart's Army Lists are in class WO 211.

Officer's records of service
Two main groups of these records are held by the Public Record Office, those compiled by the War Office and those kept by the Regimental Records Offices.

A systematic set of records of officer's service was not kept at the War Office until the second decade of the 19th century. The authorities had, until then, relied mainly on Regimental Records Offices. There were, however, five series of Statements of Service compiled in the years 1809 to 1810, 1828, 1829, 1847, and 1870 to 1872. These were based on returns made by officers themselves.

The above returns were compiled in various ways:

The series made between 1809 to 1810 is arranged alphabetically and gives details of military service only. It is located under WO 25/744-748.

The series compiled during 1828 came from returns made by officers, either retired or on half pay. This set is arranged alphabetically and gives the officer's age at commission, the dates of marriages, and births of children, as well as the officer's military service. This series is located under WO 25/749-779.

The third series in 1829 is compiled of returns from serving officers, arranged by regiments, and gives the same information as the second series. It may be located under WO 25/780-805.

The fourth series, compiled in 1847, came from retired officers and is arranged alphabetically, giving the same information as in the second series. It is located under class WO 25/808-823.

The fifth series, mainly from 1870 to 1872, has a few sets of statements which are either earlier or later than these dates. The series is arranged by the years of return and then by regiment. It is located in the class WO 25/824-870.

Following the passing of the War Office Act by the British Parliament in 1870 the system of purchasing commissions was finally abolished. A register was compiled of all officers who were holding a commission on 1 November 1871 and is kept among the Army Purchase Commission Papers in the class WO 74. There is also a series of applications from officers who were serving in both the British and Indian establishments to which certificates of service are attached. Neither series includes personal details.

Officer's records of service were kept by Regimental Record Offices and those that were eventually transferred to the War Office are located under class WO 76. Arranged by regiments they relate to events from 1755 to 1954. The kind of information given varies but it does tend to increase in quantity during the 19th century. There are two main exceptions to the above. One concerns officers of the Royal Garrison Regiment from 1901 to 1905 whose records are located under class WO 19, and, what may be of interest to Australian researchers, those of the Gloucester Regiment 1792 to 1866, are in class WO 67/24-27. The 28th (North Gloucester) Regiment served in the Australian colonies between 1835 and 1842 and a number of its officers left the Army to settle in Australia. There are a few regimental records of service kept in the class WO 25.

Artillery and Engineer officers
The records of service for Artillery officers between 1777 and 1870 are included among the regimental series in WO 76. An earlier series dating between 1727 and 1751 are kept in WO 54/684.

Returns of Engineer officers are in WO 54 also; for the years between 1786 and 1850 in WO 54/248-259; and records of service between 1796 and 1922 are in WO 25/3913-3919.

There was an additional series compiled in the mid-19th century in the Ordnance Office In-Letters kept under WO 44/686-694.

Miscellaneous series
Some further particulars of officers may be found in the documents in support of applications and submissions to the sovereign for appointments, promotions and resignations between the years 1793 and 1870. These are in WO 31.

The supporting documents often include statements of service, certificates of baptism, and marriage, death or burial from 1755 to 1908 (which have been extracted from War Office papers and files) and are in WO 42; some additional certificates are in WO 32/8903-8920. Other papers from which the certificates in WO 42 were originally extracted relate to individual officers. Officers' official notifications of marriages for the years between 1799 and 1882 are under WO 25/3239-3245.

There are a number of selected personal files, mainly concerning senior officers for the years from 1830 to 1963, which may be found in class WO 138. Also Inspection Returns recorded from 1750 to 1857 which give presence or absence of officers from their regiments at the time of the inspection. These may include brief records of service. These are found in class WO 27/489. The presence or absence of officers are also recorded in the Monthly Returns from 1759 to 1865 in WO 17.

Half pay

The system of half pay was first established in 1641 for officers of reduced or disbanded regiments. In time half pay became a kind of retaining fee. It was paid to an officer so long as he held his commission and was, in theory at least, available for future service. There are Lists, Ledgers and Registers of officers on half pay. Lists of those entitled to half pay between 1713 and 1809 are arranged by regiment in WO 24/660-747; there is a similar list of the British American forces, 1783 and 1813 in WO 24/748-762. There are further nominal lists, 1712 and 1856 in WO 25/2979-3002; these include some warrants for half pay from 1763. In 1854 a circular was sent to officers on half pay requesting details of their fitness for service; these are in WO 25/3009-3012. There are further lists relating to half pay officers in WO 25/3003-3008 and WO 25/3013-3019.

Ledgers recorded the issue of half pay and those which apply to the years 1737 to 1921 are in PMG 4; until 1841 the ledgers are arranged by regiments and are not indexed. From 1841 they are arranged alphabetically by name. The assignment of the pay, the sale of the commission, and the death of the officer are noted in the ledgers and from 1837 addresses are given. Later volumes give the date of birth.

The Commissariat was not under the control of the War Office but was a department of the Treasury. Officer's records for this branch of the service are kept under Paymaster General's Department (PMG). The years 1834 to 1835 are in class PMG 5.

Before 1857 officers of the Artillery and Engineers came under the control of the Board of Ordnance and their ledgers are kept in PMG 12 for the years 1834 to 1857. Those for foreign officers, 1822 to 1885, are in PMG 6. In PMG 7 is a further series for foreign officers which consists mainly of those who served with the King's German Legion.

Registers of half pay officers are found in WO 23. There is a series of alphabetical registers of officers in receipt of half pay for the years 1858 to 1859 and 1879 to 1880 which includes name, regiment, date of commencement, rate of pay, and a record of payments. The date of death is often noted. These are in WO 23/75-78 and are continued for the years 1880 to 1881 to 1893 to 1894 which are in WO 23/68/74. Registers for Artillery and Engineer officers on half pay are kept for the years 1810 to 1880 in WO 23/82. Those for officers of foreign regiments are in WO 23/79 to 81 which apply to the years 1858 to 1876.

Retirement and pensions for officers

One of the conditions under which an officer purchased his commission was that he was not entitled to a pension by right. An officer who wished to retire could either sell his commission, thereby recouping his capital investment, or he could go on half pay.

During the 18th century any surplus on the half pay vote was used to pay pensions to officers who were no longer fit for service.

Retirement on full pay

Few officers were entitled to retire on full pay and according to the Public Record Office this was mainly granted to those who raised a veteran or invalid company. This might be of particular interest to Australians researching the lives of officers of the Veteran Company, New South Wales. These were mainly former members of the New South Wales Corps, later the 102nd Regiment, and they returned to serve in Australia until their disbandonment in 1823.

Registers of those who retired on full pay are included in WO 23/66-82. The ledgers of payment for the years 1813 to 1896 are in PMG 3.

Pensions for wounded officers

Registers of officers who received pensions for wounds date from 1812 until 1892; these are in class WO 23/83-92. Ledgers for the payment of such pensions covering the years 1814 to 1920 are in the class PMG 9. There is also a special series for foreign officers for the years 1822 to 1885 in PMG 6 and PMG 7.

Ledgers of payment to commissariat officers for the years 1834 to 1855 are kept in PMG 5 and for ordnance officers for the years 1836 to 1857 are in PMG 12.

Widow's pension

Although officers had no entitlement to a pension for themselves there had been provisions for pensions for the widows of those killed on active service since 1708. At first the pension payment was made from a fund created by placing two fictitious men in every company or troop; later it came from an annual grant. From 1818 fifteen annuities were also paid from a fund which had been established by the will of

Colonel John Drouly. These were paid each year to the widows of officers whose annual income did not exceed £30.

Registers of those who received widows' pensions and Drouly annuities between the years 1815 to 1892 are in WO 23/88-92 and WO 23/105-113.

Ledgers of the payments of widows' pensions and Drouly annuities for the years 1713 to 1829 are in WO 24/804-883 and ledgers 1808 to 1920 are in the class PMG 11, with the exception of those from April 1870 to March 1882 which are in PMG 10.

Ledgers for pensions paid to the widows of foreign officers, for the years 1822 to 1885, are in PMG 6 and PMG 7.

Those for the widows of commissariat officers, for the years 1810 to 1855, are in PMG 5 and those for ordnance officers' widows are in PMG 12 and cover the years 1836 to 1875.

Soldier's records

Enlisted soldiers were formerly referred to as 'rank and file' but more recently they have become known as 'other ranks'. Their personal records may be traced in six main categories and these are:

1 Records of Service
2 Description Book
3 Returns of Service
4 Pay Lists and Muster Rolls
5 Casualty returns
6 Pension records

The Public Record Office holds records of service *only for men discharged before 1914*. With the exception of those who served in the artillery and ordnance (Engineers), for reasons that will be given later, *only the records of service of those who were discharged with a pension* have survived.

Records of soldiers who were discharged after 1914 onward are held by the Ministry of Defence but the majority of the World War I records were destroyed or irreparably damaged by enemy action in 1942.

Information held by the Ministry of Defence can be released only to the soldier's next of kin.

The most detailed set of records are the attestation and discharge documents; these form a class known as WO 97 (Soldier's Documents). These give a record of the man's service and, with few exceptions, give his place of birth, his age on enlistment, and a

Privates.	Period for which Payment has been made.		No. of Days.			No. of days on board Ship.	Reasons of Absence at the 1st Muster. (When Men are Absent)
	From	To	at 9d. per Diem.	at 6d. per Diem.	at 7d. per Diem.		
Brought forward····	··········	·········					
[illegible]							
Davies _[illegible]_							
Davis _Richard_			92				
Dawson _Benjamin_			92				Norfolk _[illegible]_
Deas _George_					92		
Dee _Denis_					92		_[illegible]_
Dee _Thomas_					92		_[illegible]_
Deanty _John_				92			_[illegible]_
Dean _John_			92				_[illegible]_
Dennis _John_				92			
Devenny _Patrick_			92				_[illegible]_
Dickens _William_				92			
Dicker _Henry_			92				_[illegible]_
Dinsmore _John_					92		
Diranny _Thomas_					92		_[illegible]_
Doherty _George_					92		_[illegible]_
Dooglue _Daniel_					92		_[illegible]_
Donnagtun _Daniel_					92		Bathurst
Danaghue _Timothy_					92		_[illegible]_
Doe _John_					92		Bathurst

Pay and Muster Roll of the 39th Regiment dating from 1 October 1831 to 31 December 1831, showing the privates whose names start with D. It also gives the number of days for which each man is entitled to pay, and at what rate, and where he is stationed at each monthly muster. These Rolls are arranged in annual volumes and were completed each quarter. At the end of each quarter may be found other information such as 'Men becoming non-effective', which shows the names of men who were discharged during the quarter. These lists usually give the man's date of discharge, date of birth, place of birth, and civil occupation and are often the only source of such information physical description. Details of marriage and children appear only from 1882.

These documents fall into three series:

1   Only the documents of soldiers who were discharged to a pension between the years 1756 and 1872. These are arranged by regiment and the names are listed alphabetically. For any research into this class of documents it is essential to know the man's regiment.* Records of those who served with the Royal Artillery and Royal Corps of Sappers and Miners are included from 1856 and those of members of the Royal Horse Artillery from 1864 only.

2   Those who were discharged between 1873 and 1882 and went on pensions make up this series. The documents are arranged alphabetically by name for Cavalry, Artillery, Infantry and Corps.

3   This series holds documents of soldiers who were either discharged to pension, or for other reasons such as enlistment for a limited period or discharge by purchase between the years 1883 and 1913.

Until 1855 personnel of the Artillery and corps of Sappers and Miners were under the control of the Board of Ordnance and their records were kept separately. Records of service of men who served with the Royal Artillery between 1791 and 1855 and with the Royal Horse Artillery from 1803 until 1863 include the following details:

Attestation papers which show name, age, description, place of birth, civilian occupation, dates of service, promotion, marriage, and the date of discharge or death. These documents are to be found under WO 69 and are arranged in order of the unit in which the soldier last served. These can be traced from indexes and posting books in WO 69/779-782. There is also a set of miscellaneous records of service of NCOs and Privates of the Artillery, Sappers, Miners, and civilian employees of the Board of Ordnance in WO 44/695-700. These are arranged alphabetically among the Ordnance Office In-letters.

---

* If the man's regiment is not known searchers can deduce the approximate year of his arrival from sources such as death certificates, marriage certificates, or family birth certificates. It would then be necessary to consult the Military Returns in the Returns of the Colony (Blue Books) or the Monthly Returns under WO 17. Both sources will give the regiments that were stationed in a particular part of Australia or New Zealand at that period.

Description Books

These give a physical description of the soldier, his age on enlistment, or when the book was compiled, his civilian occupation, and dates of service. The description usually consisted of the man's height, the colour of his eyes and hair, and the shape of his face.

These are arranged in regimental volumes and the soldiers' names are listed alphabetically and cover the period 1756 until 1900. They could be found in WO 25/266-688 but the majority of the volumes only cover the first-half of the 19th century.

Description Books kept by depots between 1768 and 1908 are held in WO 67.

For the Royal Artillery there are Description Books for the years 1749 to 1863 in WO 54/260-309 and for the years 1773 to 1876 in WO 69/74-80. Those for the Royal Irish Artillery are in WO 69/620 for the years 1756 to 1774 only. There are also Description Books for Sappers and Miners and Artificers for the years 1756 to 1883 in WO 69/310-316.

Soldier's records of service (pensioners)

Additional series:

A series of documents similar to those kept in WO 97 for men discharged between 1787 and 1813, and who were awarded out-pensions from the Royal Hospital, Chelsea, are in the class WO 121/1-136 and are arranged in chronological order; there is a further series of certificates for service in invalid and veteran units from 1782 to 1833 which is under WO 121/137-222, along with a register of discharges from 1871 to 1884, under WO 121/223-257.

Certificates for soldiers who were given deferred pensions are under WO 131.

For the many British Army pensioners in Ireland the hospital at Kilmainham, near Dublin, provided the same services as the Chelsea hospital. The documents of men who were awarded their pensions by the Kilmainham Board may be found in WO 119 for the years 1783 to 1822. There is also a series which covers the years from 1704, when the hospital was established, to 1922 when the Irish Free State was politically separated from Britain. This series may be found under WO 118.

For pensions that were awarded by the Commissioners of the Royal Hospital, Chelsea, there are two series of Admission Books. One which covers pensions for disability from the years 1715 to 1882 is in

WO 116 and pensions awarded for length of service from 1823 to 1902 is under WO 117.

There is a special series of Admission Books for pensioners of the Royal Artillery between 1833 and 1913 in WO 116/125-185. In each case the Admission Books give the date of examination, a brief record of service, the disability, place of birth, and a physical description.

The Chelsea Admission Books for the years 1830 to 1844 are duplicated by registers for the years 1830 to 1844 where the intended place of residence is given and for the final seven years (1838 to 1844) are indexed.

Before 1842 Army pensioners were paid by local officials such as excise officers but after that year the payment became the responsibility of Staff Officers of Pensions. These were appointed to each of the districts into which the United Kingdom was divided for this purpose. Staff Officers were required by the War Office to send in Monthly Returns which recorded the names of pensioners who had either moved into or out of the district, and of those whose pensions had ceased or who had died.

These returns are kept under WO 22 and will give the man's name, regiment, date of admission to pension, his rank, and the district from which he has moved.

The returns from British payment districts ceased in 1862 but those made to pensioners overseas and in the colonies extend until into the 1880s.

Special groups (out-pensioners)

Ordnance pensions

These were dealt with separately until 1833 in the class WO 54/388-493 in registers of ordnance pensioners being paid in 1834, the year that they were transferred to the Royal Hospital, Chelsea. These are in WO 23/141-145.

From 1780 to 1820 a number of foreign regiments were raised to serve as a part of the British Army, particularly for service in the Napoleonic wars. The largest group in this category was the King's German Legion which operated between the years 1801 and 1815. A register of pensioners from this unit is in WO 23/135.

In-pensioners

Records of the Royal Hospital, Chelsea, began in 1702 and have been subjected to a number of changes in the manner in which they are kept.

Muster Rolls for the years between 1702 and 1789 are in the classes WO 23/124-131. A register kept alphabetically for 1872 in WO 23/146; a list of in-pensioners for the years 1795 to 1813 in WO 23/134 and Admission Rolls and Books, are arranged chronologically, from 1824 to 1917 under WO 23/162-172 and 174-180. These give a man's regiment, age, service, rate of pension, and reason of discharge.

PART TWO

How to use the records of the Imperial period — a complete list of the regiments and corps stationed in Australia between 1788 and 1870 — arrival and departure dates — locations — some details of genealogical interest — the events leading to the departure of the British troops in 1870 — their records which are available in Australia and New Zealand — outline of the Maori wars — corps raised for service and settlement in New Zealand

Unidentified officer of the 99th (Lanarkshire) Regiment from a daguerreotype taken in Australia c. 1850

The Imperial period

Using the available records

The Imperial period
It is possible to employ a professional searcher to help trace a military ancestor who arrived in Australia during the Imperial period, 1788 to 1870. The Public Record Office in London maintains a panel containing the names of persons who specialise in a particular area of military record-keeping. Names and addresses are supplied on request.

For the researcher wishing to work locally a National or State Library yields results. If the ancestor in question were a Commissioned Officer, the Army Lists, published annually, contain the names of officers arranged on a regimental basis. Each volume has a general index if the officer's regiment is unknown. The Royal Marines are included in the official Army Lists and these will show an officer's rank, dates of commissioning in the Army, and in his Regiment. It will also show if the regiment served on an overseas station. The Army Lists published by Hart (from 1840) include the location of regimental depots and give details of an officer's service and medals.

Officer's personal records which are kept at the Public Record Office usually contain few personal details especially in those kept before 1829. An officer granted land or employed by a colonial government could possibly be traced through a search at a National or State Archives Office.

A military ancestor who served in the ranks may require more effort to be traced but having done so, the way is usually open to a good deal of personal information. From the moment of enlistment a complete description of the soldier was noted along with his place of birth and birth date, and his former occupation. Where the soldier's regiment is known then the researcher is indeed fortunate because the Pay and Muster Rolls will show approximately when he arrived, his progress during his service in the colonies, where he was stationed, how he was employed, and when or why he was discharged.

The Pay and Muster Rolls are among a series of Army Records that have been microfilmed by the Australian Joint Copying Project (AJCP) and are available at all National and State libraries. These Pay and Muster Rolls were completed every quarter, usually around the 24th of the month. They were bound into annual volumes and the original copies are held by the Public Record Office in London. The names of officers and Non-Commissioned Officers are listed in order of rank and the private soldiers are listed alphabetically. In addition to the Pay and Muster sheets there are other documents such as the paymaster's declarations, stoppages of pay for imprisonment, or time spent in hospital. Frequently there is a useful slip of paper which gives the particulars of men who were discharged during the previous quarter.

Each pay sheet shows the number of days that each man was entitled to pay, where he was stationed at the time of the Monthly Muster, and how he was employed other than on normal guard duty. Many of the earlier sets of rolls can be difficult to read as the ink may have faded, the paper may have become stained, and sometimes the binding of the volumes makes it impossible to photograph some of the sheets. In later chapters of this work the numbers of the microfilms are given at the conclusion of the notes on the various regiments.

If the regiment of the ancestor is unknown then it would be some help to know at what period he arrived. To find out when a particular regiment or corps arrived or departed it would be necessary to look at the Returns of the Colony or in the Monthly Returns which have been included in the AJCP. The former for New South Wales have been put on microfiche and are available at many of the larger public libraries. They cover the years 1823 to 1851 and give the names and locations of officers and their colonial appointments, if any, the titles of the regiments serving in the colony at the end of each year and the number of rank and file. The AJCP microfilms give the military returns on a monthly basis and will enable a researcher to pin-point the time of arrival more accurately and to determine the location of the troops. These are available for the following colonies and periods:

New South Wales	1790 to 1854
Western Australia	1837 to 1865
All Australian colonies	1854 to 1865
New Zealand	1849 to 1865
Engineers for New South Wales and Tasmania	1849 to 1865

When the subject's regiment is unknown and no family details are available, knowing the colonies he was stationed in is useful information as regiments remained in one or two regions. The 40th served almost all of its first tour of duty in Van Diemen's Land, while the 63rd was divided between Van Diemen's Land and Western Australia. The 43rd, 68th, and 70th served only in New Zealand. An unusual case is that of the 14th which, after spending nearly seven years of active service in the Maori wars, passed the next three years in the city of Melbourne. The official history of the 14th tells how both the officers and the rank and file were 'entertained by the colonists with cricket matches, picnics and horse racing'.

There are other useful documents which have been microfilmed by the AJCP such as the Embarkation and Disembarkation Returns. These show only the names of officers, and not all the regiments that served in Australia or New Zealand are listed. This return is under WO 25/3502 and is on reel number 1303. There is also part of the Muster Master General's Index of Casualties which shows information such as the date of a man's discharge, death, desertion or transfer which may not be available in any other source. This is under WO 25/1342 and is on reel number 1302.

Details of Army pensioners who served as warders on the convict ships that landed in Western Australia between 1862 and 1867 are on reel number 3918. Between 1849 and 1851 there were official proposals regarding the discharge of troops in Australia and New Zealand; these are on reel number 1506.

British regiments and corps stationed in Australia

Regimental titles current at the period are shown below:

Marines (four companies)	1788-1791
Royal Marines 1803-1812; 1824-1829; 1837-1854; 1862-1870	
New South Wales Corps	1791-1809
102nd Regiment of Foot	1809-1810
73rd Regiment of Foot (1st Battalion)	1810-1814
46th (South Devonshire) Regiment of Foot	1814-1818
48th (Northamptonshire) Regiment of Foot	1817-1824

3rd (East Kent, the Buffs) Regiment of Foot	1823-1827
40th (2nd Somersetshire) Regiment of Foot	1825-1829
57th (West Middlesex) Regiment of Foot	1825-1832
39th (Dorsetshire) Regiment of Foot	1827-1832
63rd (West Suffolk) Regiment of Foot	1829-1833
17th (Leicestershire) Regiment of Foot	1830-1836
4th (King's Own) Regiment of Foot	1832-1837
50th (Queen's Own) Regiment of Foot	1833-1841
21st (Royal North British) Fusiliers	1833-1839
28th (North Gloucestershire) Regiment of Foot	1835-1842
80th (Staffordshire Volunteers) Regiment of Foot	1837-1844
51st (King's Own Yorkshire) Light Infantry	1838-1846
96th Regiment of Foot	1841-1848
99th (Lanarkshire Volunteers) Regiment of Foot	1842-1856
58th (Rutlandshire) Regiment of Foot	1844-1847
11th (North Devonshire) Regiment of Foot	1845-1857
65th (2nd Yorkshire, North Riding) Regiment of Foot	1846-1849
40th (2nd Somersetshire) Regiment of Foot, 2nd tour	1846-1849
12th (East Suffolk) Regiment of Foot	1854-1861
77th (East Middlesex) Regiment of Foot	1857-1858
50th (Queen's Own) Regiment of Foot, 2nd tour	1866-1869
14th (Buckinghamshire) Regiment of Foot	1866-1869
18th (Royal Irish) Regiment of Foot	March 1870-September 1870

Short stay regiments
Between 1815 and 1819 the following regiments were in camp at Sydney while in transit from England to India:
  1st (Royal Scots) Regiment of Foot
  80th (Staffordshire Volunteers) Regiment of Foot
  86th (Royal County Down) Regiment of Foot
  84th (York and Lancaster) Regiment of Foot
In 1846 a company of Horse Artillery was held at Sydney while in transit from England to New Zealand.

Royal Artillery
Companies and batteries served in Australia from 1858 to 1870.

Royal Engineers
Officers were stationed in Australia from 1835 to 1870; the rank and file from 1857 to 1870.

Royal Corps of Sappers and Miners
Rank and file only commanded by officers of the Royal Engineers. Those who were still serving in 1857 transferred into the Royal Engineers.

Royal Staff Corps
No. 3 Company served in Australia from 1826 to 1829; the first rank
and file members began arriving late in 1825.

New South Wales Veteran Company
Raised in 1810 from men of the 102nd Regiment who were over the
age of thirty-five. They were disbanded in 1823.

Royal New South Wales Veteran Companies
Three companies were raised in 1825 and were disbanded over a
period beginning in 1829 and ending in 1833.

The Marines in Australia, 1788 to 1791; 1803 to 1812; 1824 to 1829; 1836 to 1849; 1862 to 1870

Four companies of Marines accompanied the First Fleet to New South
Wales in 1788. This branch of the service was probably chosen
because its men were accustomed to shipboard life over long periods.
Although still a part of the Regular Army Marines came under the
control of the Admiralty in 1747. The First Fleet men were all volunteers and were drawn from the Royal Naval Divisions that were
stationed at Chatham, Plymouth and Portsmouth. They were
engaged for a term of three years that was to commence with their
arrival at Botany Bay. Some details of the Marines, early service in
New South Wales is dealt with in Part 1 of this work.

The First Fleet Marines finally handed over their duties to the New
South Wales Corps early in 1792 and those who had not elected to stay
in the colony sailed for England.

By 1804 a detachment was to return, now known as Royal Marines,
and was posted to Hobart where it remained until November 1812.
The detachment carried out guard duties at most of the settlements in
the southern part of Van Diemen's Land while the northern part of the
island was garrisoned by companies of the New South Wales Corps.
They were based around the entrance of the Tamar River where the
city of Launceston stands today but was formerly known as Port
Dalrymple. When the Royal Marines left Hobart to return to
England forty-two of their number, many married, chose to remain as
settlers. On 10 December 1824 a party of Royal Marines was stationed
on Melville Island at a small settlement known as Fort Dundas where
it remained until 31 December 1829.

Seven years later a detachment of Royal Marines was stationed in
Australia, this time at Port Essington; by December 1844 the strength
of the detachment was increased to fifty-six of all ranks including one

assistant surgeon. In 1845 this force was relieved by a detachment fresh from England which consisted of two subalterns, one assistant surgeon, and forty-five rank and file. It was reported that the Port Essington settlement could not keep itself in fresh vegetables and was abandoned on 30 November 1849. The Royal Marines sailed in HMS *Meander.* In 1862 Marines returning to Australia were stationed at a small settlement at Cape York. The duties of the military force included aiding distressed crews from wrecked ships in the area. The strength of this detachment was gradually reduced to one sergeant and fourteen Marine Privates when the Imperial troops were withdrawn in 1870.

Location of Royal Marine records

Most of the records that are of biographical or genealogical interest are held at the Public Record Office at Kew near London. These include Description Books. Although they cover years from 1750 to

1888 there are many gaps with variations in the amount of information they contain. With the advent of short engagements and improved conditions the rate of desertion fell and the need for Description Books was lessened.

Attestation Form. 1780 to 1883.

Registers of Service. From 1842 to 1905.
Some records of the First Fleet Marines and the Royal Marines in Australia between 1803 and 1812 are to be found in AJCP reel number 412.

Shoulder belt plate of an officer of Royal Marines c.1850. Formerly part of collection by the Wilson family of Inverell, NSW

New South Wales Corps and 102nd Regiment of Foot, 1789 to 1810

This Corps was specially raised for permanent service in New South Wales in 1789. Recruitment was carried out at London and Chatham and recruits were often serving soldiers who were in trouble with the authorities. A few were old soldiers with service in the American War of Independence. During the Corps' service in Australia a number of recruits were accepted locally; many were the sons of men serving, a few were free settlers but many were former convicts. Much has been written about the New South Wales Corps and the way that its officers exploited both the civil and military populations by monopolising trading in the colony. A number of them obtained vast areas of land as grants, amassed fortunes and established pastoral dynasties.

A number of New South Wales Corps officers were implicated in the overthrow of Governor Bligh in 1808 and were later sent to England to be tried by court-martial. Because the Corps had been involved in what could be termed a mutiny, the authorities decided to redesignate it as the 102nd Regiment of Foot before it was sent back to England for service elsewhere. In June 1809 the New South Wales Corps officially became the 102nd Regiment of the Line and began to move from the various outstations back to Sydney. On 25 April 1810 the officers and men who had elected to stay in the Army left Australia in the *Hindostan, Dromedary,* and the *Porpoise.*

A large proportion of both officers and rank and file members of the New South Wales Corps and 102nd Regiment settled in Australia. Many of the earlier members can be traced through land grant records at State Archives Offices and, in addition to the men who transferred to the 73rd, about 100 of the older men joined the Veteran Company when it was formed in 1810.

Fortunately for genealogists who are working on the New South Wales Corps and 102nd Regiment there are many useful military records available in Australia and New Zealand. The *Description Book* from 1808 to 1814 has survived and the original is kept at the Public Record Office, at Kew. It has been microfilmed by the AJCP and is available in all the National and State libraries of Australia and New Zealand. The original volume number is WO 25/642 and the microfilm reel number is 1302.

The Pay and Muster Rolls for the New South Wales Corps and 102nd Regiment are in volumes 11028 for the years 1789 to 1797; 9399 to 9905 for the years 1798 to 1812. The microfilm reel numbers run from 412 to 416.

Many of the officers who settled in Australia became prominent members of early colonial society and have been written up in a number of the standard biographical reference works.

For example the *Australian Dictionary of Biography* D. Pike (ed.), Melbourne: Melbourne University Press, 1967, lists at least 102 military men in the volumes which cover the years 1788 to 1850. They

Subaltern, 73rd Regiment, c.1810   *Quartermaster Sergeant, NSW Corps,*
c.1805

include all ranks from Lieutenant-General Sir Maurice Charles O'Connell, who served as Lieutenant-Governor of New South Wales, to Private William Faithfull, who became a rich and influential landowner.

American War of Independence, 1776 to 1783

Civilian and military personnel who settled in New South Wales as early as the 1790s are known to have served with the British forces in the American War of Independence and some records of these are available. Although the Pay and Muster Rolls are held at the Public Record Office, the discharge certificates of men who were discharged in North America can only rarely be traced.

The Loyalist Regimental Rolls (Provincial Troops) are held at the Public Archives Office of Canada in Ottawa.

The Veteran Company, New South Wales, 1810 to 1823

In a General Order dated 29 January 1810, Governor Macquarie called for volunteers, under thirty-five, to transfer from the 102nd into the 73rd Regiment. The majority of those who wished to stay in the colony were over thirty-five and they were given the opportunity to join the Veteran Company of New South Wales. On 10 April 1810 the Governor sent a dispatch to England which included the following:

> A great Number of Old Soldiers of the 102nd who have served long in the Colony, wishing to remain in it on Account of Connexions they have formed with Convict Women by whom they had children, I have taken the Responsibility upon Myself of forming them into an Invalid or Veteran Company for the service of the Colony, until His Majesty's Pleasure be known; and I trust Your Lordship will be pleased to move the King to be so graciously pleased to approve of the Measure. I have made the Establishment of the Invalid Company One Hundred Rank and File with the usual Proportion of Serjeants and Drummers, to be under the Command and Charge of an officer of the 73rd until I shall receive orders from home respecting it.

During 1811 three former officers of the 102nd Regiment were appointed to the Veteran Company while some time later a former officer of the 73rd joined the Company.

For much of its service the Veteran Company was detailed for light duties and was stationed at Windsor, New South Wales. It was finally disbanded in September 1823 and the *Sydney Gazette* reported a few days later that 'four chose to return to the United Kingdom whereas the remainder expressed the wish to be interred where their best years were spent'.

Locations of the records of the Veteran Company, New South Wales

Very few of the officers' service records have survived. Settling in Australia, many of the officers became prominent citizens and feature in Australian biographical works of reference.

About ninety of the rank and file stayed to settle and seventy-four of these were granted land, though most of them were too old to work it.

Many of the soldiers of the Veteran Company had served at the time when the Description Book of the 102nd was kept, and this is a useful source of biographical material.

The Pay and Muster Rolls have been microfilmed for the years 1810 to 1823 and the reel numbers are 417 and 418.

See L. M. Mowle's book *Genealogical History of Pioneer Families* (Adelaide: Rigby, 1978) — a valuable reference.

73rd Regiment of Foot, 1810 to 1814

When the 73rd Regiment arrived in New South Wales with Governor Macquarie in January 1810 it became the first of thirty British infantry regiments to serve a tour of duty in Australia and New Zealand. Formerly a Highland regiment, the 73rd was transferred to the English establishment in April 1809 to encourage recruitment because of the current aversion to the Highland dress in England and southern Scotland. At this time the Regiment was much under strength but before sailing for the penal colony of New South Wales it took reinforcements from the county militias of Durham, London, and Staffordshire. When the 73rd arrived for a four-years' tour of duty there were very few of the old soldiers who had served with Lachlan Macquarie in the south India campaign.

Both the officers and the rank and file were mostly young and inexperienced. Few were able to quit the Army to settle with the possible exception of the members of the Governor's Bodyguard which transferred to the 48th Regiment soon after its arrival in 1817. The 73rd main party left for Ceylon (Sri Lanka) on 24 March 1814 after embarking in the *General Hewitt* and the *Windham*; the rear party of the Regiment sailed in January 1815 in the *General Brown* and the brig *Kangaroo*.

In 1862 the 73rd Regiment returned to the Highland establishment to become the 73rd (Perthshire) Regiment and following the Cardwell reforms of 1881 it became the 2nd Battalion of the Black Watch.

Locations of records of the 73rd Regiment

The officers' Statements of Service are available only if officers were still serving after 1829. These would be held at the Public Record Office at Kew. The personal service documents of NCOs and Privates would be at the Public Record Office only if they served long enough to receive a pension. The Regimental Description Book for the period 1810 to 1814 has not survived.

The Pay and Muster Rolls for the period 1808 to 1815 are available on microfilm in all National and State libraries in Australia and New Zealand; the reel numbers are 3868 to 3870.

The 73rd retained a company at its depot in the United Kingdom for recruiting purposes. Also a second battalion of the Regiment was raised and fought at the Battle of Waterloo and was disbanded soon after the armistice in 1816.

46th (South Devonshire) Regiment of Foot, 1814 to 1818

The early years of the Napoleonic wars saw bitter fighting in the French West Indies and it was here that the 46th suffered heavy casualties, mainly from tropical disease. The depleted 46th returned to the United Kingdom to re-equip and reinforce at a time when the best of new recruits were being posted to the campaign in the Peninsula. Those destined for a four-year tour of duty in New South Wales, to be followed by thirty years in India, were on the whole well below the usual standard. They were undersize, many were under-age, and the Description Book of the time shows that they were mostly pale and thin.

The first divisions of the 46th disembarked at Sydney early in the February of 1814 from the *Windham* and the *General Hewitt*. The last detachment to arrive was the rear party on 27 January 1815. At this time the 46th, which normally drew most of its recruits from the western counties of England, was a very mixed unit. Rather less than half of the rank and file were English; of the remainder many were Irish, and the rest Scottish. Many of the most experienced senior NCOs were men who had transferred from the 73rd.

Only a few of the 46th officers or soldiers are known to have settled

Regimental medal awarded to private John Horrocks of the 48th Regiment in 1819 during his service in Australia

in Australia. The Regiment's Quartermaster* returned from India to supervise the business enterprises he had established in Sydney and a time-expired sergeant clerk took up employment in the Government Office. The latter was to become well known as a Wesleyan Methodist preacher.†

The 46th sailed for Madras in 1818 to begin a long period of service in southern India.

In 1881 the 46th Regiment became the 2nd Battalion of the Duke of Cornwall's Light Infantry.

Locations of records of the 46th

At this period very few details of officer's service had survived but some details can be located in the Succession Registers which may be

---

* Hugh Macdonald.
† James Scott.

'found in WO 25. Service with other regiments can be picked up in Army Lists using the General Index.

Soldiers who were discharged with a pension are listed under WO 97 or in Description Books if genealogical information is required. Description Books may be found in the class WO 25 in volumes 266 to 688. Description Books kept at regimental depots between the years 1768 and 1908 are in WO 67. Many of the early books have not survived.

The Pay and Muster Rolls are, as in other regiments, in the class WO 12 and for the 46th Regiment for the years 1812 to 1817 the microfilm numbers are reels 3795 to 3796. Copies of these are held by all National and State libraries of Australia and New Zealand.

48th (Northamptonshire) Regiment of Foot, 1817 to 1824

Two battalions of the 48th Regiment fought in the Peninsular battles between 1808 and 1814 and because of the heavy casualties sustained the two were merged into a single battalion before coming to New South Wales.

Three companies of the 48th sailed from Cork in the *Matilda* and disembarked on 3 August 1817; the Commanding Officer, Lieutenant-Colonel J. Erskine, sailed with them and worked hard during the long voyage to keep the officers, soldiers, and their families occupied and healthy. He did much to improve the Army's image during the 48th Regiment's stay in Australia.

Because of the amalgamation of the two battalions, the 48th was over the normal regimental strength and during its service in Australia the War Office gave authority for officers with more than ten years' service to sell their commissions and settle in the colony. The rank and file were encouraged to transfer, if they wished, into the 3rd (East Kent) Regiment which began arriving in 1822.

A number of officers took advantage of the offer and many of them settled on land grants to lead pioneer colonial families. Very few men in the ranks were able to leave the Army to settle at that time but a number were able to return and settle as veterans some years later.

After seven years in New South Wales and Van Diemen's Land the 48th received orders to prepare for service in India. On 5 March 1824 the first divisions of the 48th embarked in the *Grenock*, the *Asian*, and the *Sir Godfrey Webster*.

Locations of records of the 48th

Service records of officers are difficult to locate unless they were still

DESCRIPTION, SERVICE, &c. of

| | | Regt. |

Where Born ....

When ditto. ....

Height.............

Complexion..........

Hair ....

Eyes ....

Face ....

Marks ....

Trade

Former Service in other, and what Corps .....

Attestation in present Corps. ....

Bounty. ....

When, where, and by whom paid ....

Soldier's Pay Book. Pages 1 and 4 of the Pay Book of Private Benjamin Reed of the 3rd (The Buffs) Regiment. He was discharged in January 1824 to be ... settlement where he was also parish clerk at St Thomas' church. His place of birth would have been ...

serving in 1828 when Statements of Service were required. The Registers of the Succession Rolls will show where an officer is stationed during a particular year with the names listed in order of seniority. As with other infantry regiments the records of the rank and file individual documents, which include Attestation Papers, service record and discharge papers, are under WO 97 unless the man did not receive a pension. The Pay and Muster Rolls are kept in the class WO 12 and those for the years 1814 to the end of 1824 have been microfilmed and are available in the National and State libraries of Australia and New Zealand. The reel numbers are 3796 to 3799. In 1881 the 48th Regiment became the 1st Battalion of the Northamptonshire Regiment.

3rd (East Kent, the Buffs) Regiment of Foot, 1822 to 1827

One of England's oldest regiments; it had served in the Peninsula, North America, France, and Ireland before being posted to New South Wales. Before leaving England it was divided into small detachments departing over a two-year period.

During its service in Australia the 3rd Regiment was able to claim some credit for being the first British Regiment to provide officers and soldiers to man the Mounted Police. A number of the men are known to have transferred to the incoming regiment when the 3rd was ordered to prepare to leave. Several of the officers sold their commissions to settle, including the Commanding Officer, Lieutenant-Colonel William Stewart, who retired from the Army some years later to settle on a large property in the Bathurst area.

In January 1827 the 3rd Regiment, ordered to sail for Calcutta, embarked in small detachments but were not united into a complete regiment until the following year.

Locations of records of the 3rd Regiment of Foot

Some Statements of Service for officers who were still serving after 1829 may be found at the Public Record Office under WO 25.

Soldier's Documents for those who were in receipt of a pension are under WO 97 and the surviving Description Books are under WO 25.

Records available in Australia and New Zealand which may be of genealogical interest are the Pay and Muster Rolls which are now microfilmed and held at National and State libraries. These cover the period from December 1822 until December 1827 and the reel numbers are 3694 to 3696. The Military Returns in the Colonial Records (Blue Books) are missing for the years 1822 to 1829.

40th (2nd Somersetshire) Regiment of Foot

First tour 1824 to 1829
Second tour 1852 to 1860
New Zealand 1860 to 1866

The 40th Regiment fought at Waterloo, although few of the men who took part in this battle would have been still serving when the Regiment arrived in Australia to begin its first tour of duty in 1824. On this occasion a part of the Regiment was posted to Van Diemen's Land to protect settlers from attacks by bushrangers and hostile Aborigines.

The 40th Regiment sailed in detachments for Bombay between September and December 1829. The first division, which consisted of seven officers and 172 rank and file, left on September 1829 in the *Phoenix*. On reaching the Indian Ocean the ship was becalmed for several weeks and the crew mutinied when it appeared that food and fresh water were running out. The soldiers of the 40th carried out the seamen's duties and the *Phoenix* reached Bombay in January 1830.

The 40th Regiment began its second period of garrison duty in 1852 and on this occasion its function was mainly one of defence. The transportation of convicts had ceased in New South Wales and was being phased out in Van Diemen's Land. Fears of an invasion were growing as relations with France, Russia, and the United States of America were far from good. In March 1854 Britain declared war against Tsarist Russia. The military headquarters for the Australasian colonies was moved to Melbourne at about the same time.

During its second period in Australia the 40th Regiment spent most of the time in Victoria providing armed escorts for gold being dispatched from the goldfields to Melbourne. The 40th also took part in the action against the Eureka Stockade in December 1854. One officer and five soldiers died in this uprising. In 1860 the Regiment was transferred to New Zealand to join the force being strengthened to put down the second major rebellion of the Maoris.

During this campaign the 40th were known to the New Zealand settlers as the 'Excellers' from the Roman numerals XL, for 40, that they wore on their forage caps. The Regiment took part in many of the major engagements of the second Maori war.

Locations of records of the 40th Regiment

The Public Record Office
Locations of records of the 40th Regiment in Australia: microfilms of
the Pay and Muster Rolls for the years 1823 to 1828 and 1852 to 1866.
The reel numbers are 3772 to 3774 and for the second period, 3774 to
3792. Available in the National and State libraries.

The Medal Roll for the New Zealand Medal includes personnel of
the 40th Regiment.

Locations of records of the 40th Regiment in New Zealand

The New Zealand National Libraries at both the Wellington and
Auckland branches.

In 1881 the 40th Regiment became the 1st Battalion of the South
Lancashire Regiment (The Prince of Wales Volunteers).

57th (West Middlesex) Regiment of Foot, 1825 to 1832 Australia; 1860 to 1866 New Zealand

Like the 3rd and 48th Regiments the 57th fought throughout the
Napoleonic wars and suffered heavy casualties during the Peninsular
Campaign. Of the 700 men who served with the Regiment in Aus-
tralia ninety-six had been in Wellington's battles.

The first detachment of the 57th left England in October 1824 and
the last division left Chatham in November 1825 and by mid-1826 the
entire Regiment was quartered at Sydney.

The first military detachment to serve at King George Sound was
supplied by the 57th which also posted officers and men to the new
settlement at Moreton Bay. Assigned to the Indian Establishment, the
57th sailed for Madras and the first division sailed in March 1831.

In January 1860 the 57th Regiment arrived in New Zealand in time
to take part in the second Maori war. When a party of men of the 57th
were ambushed near New Plymouth in May 1863 it was tantamount
to a declaration of war. The Regiment took part in a number of major
engagements and was stationed in the Wanganui area before being
posted back to England in 1866.

In 1881 the 57th became the 1st Battalion of the Middlesex
Regiment.

Locations of the records of the 57th Regiment

A number of officers of the 57th settled in Australia and many were to establish large and prominent families. These are, in many cases, included in Australian biographical reference works. Many officers had completed their Statements of Service in 1828 to 1829 and these may be inspected at the Public Records Office. The Pay and Muster Rolls were microfilmed for the years 1824 to 1833 and 1860 to 1867. The reel numbers run from 3816 to 3826.

No. 3 Company, Royal Staff Corps, 1825 to 1829

The Royal Staff Corps, a multi-purpose unit, was a part of the Quartermaster-General's Department enabling the War Office to exercise control over it. This was not possible with the Corps of Sappers and Miners which came under the management of the Board of Ordnance.

Towards the end of 1825 No. 3 Company, Royal Staff Corps was posted to Australia. The officers were either civil engineers or surveyors and the NCOs and Privates were skilled or semi-skilled tradesmen. The Company was divided into detachments, some in New South Wales, but the greater number were in Van Diemen's Land, centred on the township of Oatlands. Here the Royal Staff Corps men built most of the public and many of the private buildings.

It was intended that the Corps would, in part, replace a number of civilian Overseers of Convicts and thereby reduce costs. The scheme was not a success as the majority of the Royal Staff Corps men were young, inexperienced, and unable to control convict labour. The Company was ordered to disband and its members were given the option of staying in the Army to be posted elsewhere or staying in the colony as settlers. About twelve chose to continue serving and were sent to Mauritius; the remainder took their discharge and many received land grants on the same basis as the Royal Veterans. Others went into business on their own account and were given town allotments; a few became hotel licensees.

Locations of records of Royal Staff Corps

At the Public Record Office there are the Pay and Muster Rolls which cover the period from the formation of the Corps during the Napoleonic wars to the time of its disbandment in 1833. No Description Books have survived. Few, if any, soldier's Records of Service are available because most were young soldiers who did not serve long enough to qualify for a pension and few of them would have been discharged on medical grounds.

In Australia and New Zealand the microfilms of the Pay and Muster Rolls are available. The reel number is 3917 and covers the period from September 1826 to October 1829.

Royal New South Wales Veteran Companies, 1826 to 1833

At various times in its history the British Army formed what was termed 'Invalid Battalions' from pensioned soldiers who were still fit for garrison duties. From 1804 these became known as Veteran Battalions or Companies. In 1810 Governor Macquarie was able to form a Company of Veterans from the older members of the 102nd Regiment who wished to remain in Australia (*see* p. 45).

There had been some dissatisfaction among the Commanding Officers of regiments in Australia when some of their best men were seconded into the Mounted Police. Governor Brisbane had suggested that a force of permanent mounted military police be formed for the colony but no action was taken on this matter.

In 1825 the British Government authorised the formation of three Companies of Veterans for service in New South Wales and, later, in Van Diemen's Land. Preference was given to former NCOs or men who had served with the cavalry; they would be engaged for two years' service to count from their arrival in New South Wales. The rank and file were to be paid at cavalry rate, draw free rations and become entitled to a grant of land on completion of their service.

Recruiting began in September 1825 and six officers who were out on half pay from a variety of regiments were appointed to administer the nucleus of the three Companies.

Although disbandment of the Companies began in August 1829, fresh reinforcements continued to arrive from England well into 1831, and it was early in 1833 before the last men were discharged. The Royal New South Wales Veteran Companies are of particular significance to the military genealogist because of the high proportion of officers and soldiers who settled in Australia. The three Companies were stationed in New South Wales and Van Diemen's Land for over six years and during that time almost 400 officers and other ranks served with them. When the last group of men were in the process of being discharged the local press commented on the fact that only about eighty had taken advantage of the free passage back to England. Of the eight officers who served with the Companies only one returned to the United Kingdom and this for a court-martial and civil action which resulted in his imprisonment. The other officers, including a surgeon, were able to settle into government employment or

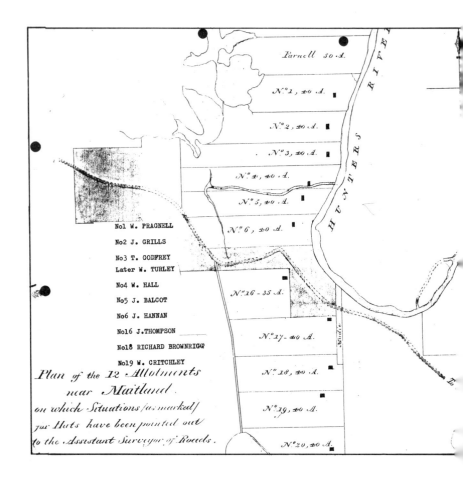

Veterans' land grants, Maitland, 1829

obtain by grant or purchase extensive areas of land. Many of their descendants are still living in Australia.

The majority of the rank and file were granted land after they were discharged. These free grants were awarded on much the same basis as those given to the Marines or the members of the Veteran Company which was disbanded in 1823. In a Memorandum dated 13 January 1829 Governor Darling added several more conditions to the regulations governing the grants for Veterans. In addition to free rations for twelve months, a set of tools for working the land, and a

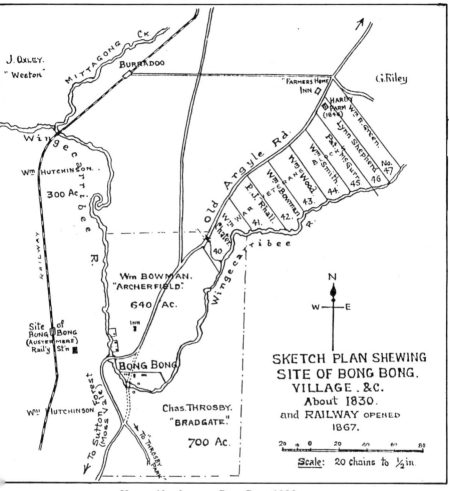

J. OXLEY.
" Weston "

BURRADOO

G. Riley

" FARMERS HOME
INN

HARDY
FARM Wm R. Green
(1848)

Wm HUTCHINSON.

300 Ac.

Wm
SHATER

Old Argyle Rd.

P. J. Rhall.
41.

Wm BOWMAN
42.
43.
Wm Wood
B. J. Smith.
Pat McGurk
44.
45.
Lynn Shepherd

No. 47
No. 46

40

Wingecarribee R.

Wm BOWMAN.
"ARCHERFIELD."

640 Ac.

N

W——E

Site of
BONG BONG
(AUSTERMERE)
Rail'y St'n

INN

BONG BONG

Wm HUTCHINSON

To Sutton Forest
(Moss Vale)

To Throsby Park

Chas. THROSBY.
"BRADGATE."

700 Ac.

SKETCH PLAN SHEWING
SITE OF BONG BONG.
VILLAGE. &C.
About 1830.
and RAILWAY OPENED
1867.

20 10 0   20   40   60   80

Scale: 20 chains to ½ in.

Veterans' land grants, Bong Bong 1829

cow for the married men, the following proposals were added. A log cabin would be built on or near the grant for the married men, the allotments would be grouped together, and each group was to include men who were skilled in different trades thereby enabling them to support their families.

The country allotments varied from forty to 100 acres (16 to 40.5 ha.) depending upon the quality of the soil and general situation of the grant. The town grants were usually a few perches in area but were sufficient to build a hut for accommodation with a little more for carrying on a trade or small business. A perch is a little over twenty-five square metres (30.25 sq. yds).

In New South Wales the country allotments were located at Bong Bong, Dapto, Goulburn, Maitland, and Wollombi. A number of Veterans became hotel licensees after they had worked their grant for the minimum period of seven years. The licensee's military associations were often reflected in the names of their hotels, such as the 'Waterloo Inn', the 'Duke of Wellington' or the 'Fortune of War'.

In Van Diemen's Land the Veterans of No. 3 Company who chose to settle did so mainly in and around urban areas. Eight were located on the banks of the Tamar on what was known as the east arm. A number requested allotments at Launceston but many settled on what was to become the outskirts of Hobart. During the mid-19th century the top end of Murray Street was known as 'Veteran's Row' and as late as the mid-1920s an elderly Hobart citizen recalled his childhood acquaintance with some of the older Veterans.

Locations of records of the Royal New South Wales Veterans

At the Public Record Office only one officer's Statement of Service has survived, that of Captain (Brevet Lieutenant-Colonel) Henry Dumaresq who commanded the three Companies between 1826 and 1829. Army Lists before 1826 give the Royal Veteran Officer's previous regiments. For other ranks, knowing their previous regiments will help to trace their personal documents. Most were in receipt of a pension, either for long service or disability. This might denote that personal documents are available. If only the man's regiment is known it may be possible to find a Description Book. These will invariably show the man's place of birth, his age, civil occupation, and the date of his enlistment. These are all held at the Public Record Ofice.

All National and State libraries in Australia and New Zealand hold copies of the Pay and Muster Rolls for the Royal New South Wales Veteran Companies for the period from June 1826 to June 1832. There are some gaps in these records mainly because the tight binding of the volumes does not allow for filming. The reel number is 3917. The New South Wales and Tasmanian State Archives Offices both hold much useful material about the Veterans. The New South Wales Archives Office has a collection of letters and other papers dealing with the Veterans' applications for land. Much of this material has been microfilmed and will sometimes give clues as to the writer's previous military service. Surveyors' maps of the allotments are also held at this office. The Tasmanian State Archives hold documents relating to the Veterans who settled there. These include correspondence from the soldiers and the officer-in-charge with much personal information including character references and previous military service.

39th (Dorsetshire) Regiment of Foot, 1825 to 1831

Before leaving the depot at Chatham the 39th Regiment was divided into eighteen detachments, the largest of these consisting of three officers and fifty-one rank and file. Most were assigned to convict transports to serve as guards; the first left in December 1825 and the last in April 1827.

The time taken to complete the voyage to Sydney varied. The *Cambridge*, which carried the Headquarters Company, took the record time of eighty-eight days; the slowest vessel took almost six months. In addition to the routine outstations in New South Wales, detachments were posted to Norfolk Island and Van Diemen's Land.

During the Dorsetshire's tour of duty in Australia there were many extensive explorations into Australia's interior and both officers and soldiers took part in these operations.

The Regiment was ordered to prepare for service in India in May 1831 but did not embark until July of the following year.

In 1881 the 39th Regiment became the 1st Battalion, the Dorsetshire Regiment.

63rd (West Suffolk) Regiment of Foot, 1829 to 1834

The HQ Company of the 63rd arrived at Sydney on 18 February 1830 and, after landing the convicts, it continued on to Hobart where the main body of the Regiment was to be stationed. One officer, two sergeants and twenty privates remained at Sydney as an outstation, and a detachment of sixty was posted to the Swan River settlement in Western Australia.

In Van Diemen's Land the 63rd Regiment was divided into small detachments and parties stationed in eighteen localities as convict guards. Many of the smaller detachments would have had only a corporal in sole charge. In a Garrison Order dated 19 December 1830, Lieutenant-Governor Sir George Arthur commended the men on the good state of their health and smart appearance in spite of the dispersed organisation of their Regiment. Authorities believed that such dispersal would have an adverse effect on the efficiency and morale of the troops.

In March 1833 the 63rd Regiment received orders to prepare to transfer to the Indian Establishment to strengthen the forces of the East India Company at Madras. The Regimental Headquarters embarked on the troopship *Lord Lyndoch* on 23 December 1833; the second division of the Regiment sailed in the *Isabella* on 28 December, and the third divsion in the *Aurora* which sailed on 1 January 1834.

In 1883 the 63rd was re-designated the 1st Battalion, the Manchester Regiment.

17th (Leicestershire) Regiment of Foot, 1830 to 1836

The HQ Company of the 17th Regiment embarked on the convict ship *York* on 17 August 1830 and after arrival in Australia was soon posted at Parramatta. Detachments were sent to most of the out-stations with a strong detachment assigned to Van Diemen's Land to protect the settlers from bushrangers and Aborigines.

In New South Wales a large force of both officers and soldiers of the 17th were seconded to the Mounted Police, and a number of officers were appointed to colonial government positions.

On 4 March 1836 the HQ Company embarked for Bombay and a second division of the Regiment departed five days' later, leaving one company behind to serve as a rear party.

The 17th (Leicestershire) Regiment was what might be termed an average infantry regiment, staying in Australia for a little over five years (an average period for a tour of duty in the Australian colonies). A computer analysis determined how many officers and rank and file members of the Regiment stayed behind when the time came for it to embark. Thirty settlers were married. The following set of figures gives the reasons, whether compulsory or voluntary.

Discharged with gratuity*	33
Discharged on payment of a fee	23
Discharged, limited service expired	5
Discharged for other reasons (? medically unfit)	3
Discharged to Out-pension (twenty-one years' service)	4
Discharged with ignominy	1
Officers retired by sale of commission	11

During the Regiment's stay twenty-four NCOs and privates died of illnesses common at the time, such as typhoid and tuberculosis. The above figures have not included deserters who were not apprehended.

---

* Men discharged before completing their engagement because of reduction of regimental strength.

4th (King's Own) Regiment of Foot, 1832 to 1837

The men of the 4th Regiment arrived in Australia in nine different ships, each carrying about one company; the first was the convict ship *Jane*, which dropped anchor in Sydney harbour in November 1831 after a voyage of six months; the second vessel was the *Glen Anderson* which arrived some days later. By late December nine of the Regiment's ten companies had arrived. The rear party did not report until January 1833, almost a year after the 4th had established its Headquarters at Parramatta in place of the 17th Regiment.

The first troops to be stationed at the new Port Phillip settlement was a detachment, thirty-two strong, of men of the King's Own. They arrived with Captain William Lonsdale in October 1836 when he was appointed as Resident Magistrate. Lonsdale was to stay and become Colonial Secretary. Victoria won self-government in 1850.

Late in 1837 all detachments of the 4th were recalled to Sydney in preparation for service in India. The advance party left in August but the main body of the Regiment embarked on 26 December 1837 and arrived at Madras on 9 April 1838.

Location of the records

Histories of the 39th, 63rd, 17th, and 4th Regiments are well documented and the records of their stay in Australia are fairly intact. The Pay and Muster Rolls include the periods the men spent at sea for both the inward and outward voyages.

Many of the officers of these Regiments stayed to become senior police officers or government officials (*see* p. 15). Even those who served as minor government officers can be traced with comparative ease in the official colonial and State records. There are numerous local press notices which are enlightening.

Pay and Muster Rolls
The AJCP microfilm reel numbers are

The 39th 3770-3772	The 17th 3748-3750
The 63rd 3839-3841	The 4th 3696-3699

50th (Queen's Own) Regiment of Foot

First tour 1883 to 1841
Second tour 1866 to 1869
New Zealand 1863 to 1866
The 50th Regiment arrived at Sydney on 21 November 1833 in charge of convicts. Soon after it disembarked three Companies were sent to

Van Diemen's Land and two to Norfolk Island; most of the Regiment remained in New South Wales.

After spending a little over six years in the Australian colonies the 50th was ordered to hold itself in readiness to embark for Bengal and on 29 January 1841 nine companies sailed in the ships *Crusader* and *Lady McNaughton*. The remaining Company embarked in the ship *Ferguson* which sailed at a date not recorded. This ship was wrecked in the Torres Straits but there were no casualties and the Company was able to join the Regiment at Fort William in Bengal.

The 50th Regiment suffered heavy casualties during the war against the Sikhs and went on to serve in the Crimean War before returning to the Australasian region to take part in the third Maori war. It disembarked at Auckland on 14 Novvember 1863.

The 50th's last engagement was to assist in the capture of Putahi Pah on 7 January 1866. Posted for a second time to New South Wales, the First Division of the Regiment embarked at Auckland on 3 October 1866 and arrived at Sydney three days later. This was considered to have been a very fast trip!

The 50th's second tour of duty in Australia was regarded by the Regiment as a rest period as they had experienced almost continuous active service since the Crimea. Quartered at the new Victoria Barracks, Sydney, both the officers and soldiers spent much time improving the facilities around the Barracks, including preparing the land for the future Sydney Cricket Ground. Detachments stationed at Brisbane, Melbourne, and Adelaide, enjoyed a similar rest period before sailing from Sydney in the *Himalaya* on 24 March 1869.

In 1881 the 50th Regiment became the 1st Battalion of the West Kent Regiment.

21st (Royal North British Fusiliers) Regiment, 1833 to 1839

Regiments of Fusiliers (formerly Fuzileers) were raised in various parts of the United Kingdom to protect artillerymen who did not carry small arms. These regiments took their names from the light pattern of musket, known as a 'fuzil', that the men were issued with.

The 21st arrived in Australia by detachments during 1832 and 1833 and were based at Hobart. The Regiment did not actually serve in New South Wales but used Sydney as a staging camp; detachments were posted to Port Phillip and the Swan River settlements.

In, addition to guarding convicts the men of the 21st in Van Diemen's Land were also allotted additional duties with the Mounted Police. Their Commanding Officer, Lieutenant-Colonel J. T. Leahy, reported that his men found these duties 'difficult, incessant and laborious and brought no honour with them'.

The 21st was a Scottish, although not Highland, Regiment which drew most of its recruits from the Glasgow area.

The Regiment left Australia in three divisions. The first embarked at Hobart in February 1839, and the second sailed from the Swan River settlement in July 1839 bound for Calcutta. The 21st served with distinction in the Afghan War and on the north-west frontier of India.

In 1877 the 21st Regiment became the Royal Scots Fusiliers.

Locations of records of the 21st Regiment

Officers should have completed their Statements of Service although details of their service in India could be missing. The Pay and Muster Rolls were microfilmed for the years 1832 to 1841 and the reel numbers are 3758 to 3763.

Royal Engineers, 1835 to 1870, Australia and New Zealand

Governor Darling and Lieutenant-Governor Arthur both appealed to the Home Government for military engineers to plan and build 'works that are necessary for the protection and security of the Colony'. No action was taken until 1835 when London sent an officer of the Royal Engineers and a detachment of the Royal Corps of Sappers and Miners. At this stage the Royal Engineers was a Staff Corps consisting of trained military or civil engineers; the latter Corps comprised only NCOs and Privates who were skilled or semi-skilled tradesmen. The two Corps were amalgamated in 1856 to become the Royal Engineers.

Between 1835 and 1870 officers and soldiers of the Royal Engineers and the Royal Corps of Sappers and Miners planned and built numerous public buildings, docks, bridges, and defence installations. Men of the Royal Corps of Sappers and Miners built and operated the Royal Mint in Sydney. At various times officers and rank and file were located at Norfolk Island, Van Diemen's Land, and all mainland colonies of Australia and New Zealand. Many were to settle permanently.

Locations of records of the Royal Engineers and the Royal Corps of Sappers and Miners

Until 1855 these two Corps were not the responsibility of the War Office but the Board of Ordnance, and records relating to them were kept separately. The Public Record Office holds a series of original Patents and Warrants of Appointment dating from 1670 until 1855. The class numbers of these books are WO 54/939-945. There is a return of engineer officers under WO 54248-259 for the years 1786 to 1850.

Description Books for Sappers and Artificers from 1756 to 1883 are under WO 69/310-316. There is also a collection of records of service and other documents of Sappers and Miners under WO 44/695-700.

Officers of the Royal Engineers are included in the Army Lists but some biographical details may be found in Hart's Army Lists from the mid-19th century.

Microfilm copies of the Pay and Muster Rolls of the above Corps are not held in Australia or New Zealand at present, but many of the men were employed on Public Works and Survey duties. Biographical details of these may be found in colonial records held by most State Archives Offices.

The Monthly Returns (WO 17) include the locations of officers of the Royal Engineers between 1835 and 1850. The reel number is 1547.

Royal Artillery, New Zealand 1846 to 1870; Australia, 1856 to 1870

Like the Royal Engineers and Royal Corps of Sappers and Miners, the Royal Artillery came under the control of the Board of Ordnance before 1856. Originally a citizen force, it became a permanent Corps in 1688 and until 1859 it was formed into battalions and companies. After 1859 it consisted of brigades and batteries. The early British regiments in Australia provided personnel to man the cannons placed at various defence points around the coast. Successive governors appealed to the authorities in London for trained gunners to be sent out but there was no response until it was decided to send a company of horse-drawn artillery to New Zealand in 1843. This company remained in transit at Sydney from November 1843 until February 1846. The first Company of Artillery did not reach Sydney until October 1856. The last battery left Sydney in September 1870. The following list shows all artillery units that served in Australia and/or New Zealand between 1843 and 1870: 2nd Company, 6th Battalion; 8th Company, 10th Battalion; 3rd Company, 7th Battalion; No. 1 Battery, 15 Brigade; No. 1 Battery, and 1 Brigade.

Records of the Royal Artillery share the same history as those of the Royal Engineers. These were not kept by the War Office but by the Board of Ordnance until 1855.

Locations of Royal Artillery records

Officers' details may be found in Army Lists and where they were stationed at a given time can be traced in Law's List of Royal Artillery. Records of Service for artillery officers from 1777 to 1870 are included in the regimental series WO 76; there is an earlier series from 1727 to 1751 in WO 54/684 at the Public Record Office. The records of service of soldiers of the artillery between 1791 and 1863 are kept with the series WO 69. These documents may include Attestation Papers which give name, age, description, place of birth, civilian occupation, dates of service, promotion, marriage, and date of discharge or death. This information is arranged in order of the last unit in which the soldier served. From indexes and posting books in WO 69/779-782 this can be ascertained.

Description Books for the Royal Artillery for the years from 1749 to 1863 and 1773 to 1876 are in WO 54/260-309.

Muster Books and Pay Lists for the Royal Artillery for the years 1708 to 1878 are under WO 10.

Locations of Royal Artillery records in Australia and New Zealand

The names of officers can be traced in the Returns of the Colonies and also a few NCOs may be found there. The latter were seconded as staff instructors and were paid out of colonial funds; this would have applied to the Australian colonies and New Zealand.

The Pay and Muster Rolls of the Royal Artillery were microfilmed as recently as 1986 and are now available at State and National libraries. The period covered is from August 1845 to June 1870 and the reel and piece numbers appear with the guide before the British Infantry regiments in the Appendix on page 143.

28th (North Gloucestershire) Regiment of Foot, 1836 to 1842

The arrival of the first elements of the 28th Regiments in Sydney was noted by the *Australian* on 23 January 1836; small parties of the Regiment had been moving in a few weeks before that date. The 28th had served in the Peninsula and at Waterloo and a few of the more senior officers who came to Australia had fought in both campaigns. Members of the 28th were noted for the distinct badge worn at the back as well as the front of the cap; this commemorated a back-to-back engagement against the French at Alexandria during the Egyptian War in 1801.

During its tour of duty in the Australian colonies the 28th Regimental Headquarters was established at Parramatta but detachments were posted to most of the military outstations. The Regimental Band, much in demand by the civilian population, was reported to have played regularly at the Domain in Sydney.

Early in 1842 an insurrection broke out in north-western India and the 28th was ordered to proceed to Bombay. When the Regiment arrived during September 1842 it was found that no arrangements had been made for its accommodation and the men were shipped by a local steamer to the port of Karachi. This part of the voyage was to prove disastrous. The steamship was overcrowded and ran into heavy monsoon rains; food and medical supplies were short and many men became seriously ill or died. On arrival at Karachi there were insufficient men to carry out normal duties and the Regiment was ordered to a rest camp in Poona to recuperate.

In 1881 the 28th joined with the 61st Regiment to become the Gloucestershire Regiment.

Locations of records of the 28th Regiment

For some inexplicable reason officers' Records of Service are kept under WO 67/24-27 at the Public Record Office. These include the years 1792 to 1866. Documents for the other ranks of the 28th, like other infantry regiments, are kept under WO 97 at the Public Record Office.

In Australia and New Zealand microfilm copies of the Pay and Muster Rolls of the 28th are held at all National and State libraries. These run from the years 1835 to 1843 and the reel numbers are 3764 to 3768.

80th (Staffordshire Volunteers) Regiment of Foot, 1836 to 1844

Before serving in Australia the 80th Regiment was stationed in Ireland following years of service in Malta. Assembling at Cork before embarkation, the Regiment was divided into seventeen detachments which were assigned to convict ships. These detachments sailed at various dates between 13 November 1836 and 18 December 1838.

The Regimental Headquarters of the 80th was first established a Sydney but was later moved to Parramatta. The Regiment provided number of officers and fifty-six of its rank and file for Mounted Polic duties. Detachments were posted to most of the stations and out stations including Norfolk Island where the men faced the task of putting down a convict riot.

In April 1840 a detachment embarked for the Bay of Islands to become the first British troops to be stationed in New Zealand. A number of these troops were present, as a military escort, at the signing of the Treaty of Waitangi. The detachment remained in New Zealand until November 1843 when it returned to Sydney to join the main body of the Regiment which was preparing to embark for India. The 80th is the only British regiment to have served in New Zealand which does not include the battle honour 'New Zealand' on its colours because it took no part in Maori wars.

After long delays the 80th Regiment marched out of the old George Street Barracks in Sydney and embarked in the vessels *Royal Saxon*, *Briton*, *Lloyd*, and *Enmore*. After lying in the harbour for three days they sailed for Calcutta on 16 August 1844. In December 1845 the Regiment suffered very heavy casualties at Ferozeshah, the deciding battle of the wars against the Sikhs.

In 1881 the 80th Regiment became the 2nd Battalion of the South Staffordshire Regiment.

Locations of records of the 80th Regiment

Many officers' personal records of service are incomplete; some do not include entries after the Regiment left Malta in 1830. There are some service details of officers who became casualties or received awards for gallantry in Hart's Army Lists. The names of the rank and file who died in the Sikh wars may be found in the Regiment's Monthly Muster Rolls under WO 12/6411 at the Public Record Office. In Australia and New Zealand the microfilm copies of the Pay and Muster Rolls are available at National and State libraries. These cover the years 1836 to 1845; the reel numbers are 3880 to 3884.

A number of NCOs and Privates of the 80th Regiment remained permanently in the Mounted Police and may still have been serving when the New South Wales Police Force was formed in 1862. Some early records are still in existence.

51st King's Own (2nd Yorkshire, West Riding) Light Infantry, 1838 to 1846

The 51st was designated as a Light Infantry Regiment in 1809 and as such it fought with distinction in most of the major battles of the Peninsular campaign and at Waterloo.

The Regiment left England by detachments, serving as convict guards, during the latter half of 1838 and the first part of 1839. Although the Headquarters was established at Sydney the main body was stationed in Van Diemen's Land. In 1840 a part of the Headquarter Company was selected to help in the establishment of a new settlement in Western Australia. On 21 October the party embarked for the Swan River and King George's Sound, consisting of two Captains, four Subalterns, one Assistant-Surgeon, six Sergeants, eight Corporals and 124 Privates.

The Regiment received orders to prepare for service in India in 1844 but owing to the disturbances in New Zealand it was detained until 8 August 1846 when the Headquarters and 500 of all ranks embarked for Bengal in the *Agincourt*. The remainder of the Regiment sailed from Hobart on 8 November 1846.

In 1881 the 51st became the 1st Battalion of the King's Own Yorkshire Light Infantry.

Locations of records of the 51st

The service records of many officers would be briefly noted in the Hart's Army Lists (from 1839) and all of them should have completed their Statements of Service which should be at the Public Record Office under WO 25.

In Australia the microfilm copies of the Pay and Muster Rolls are available at the National and State libraries; these cover the years 1837 to 1847 and the reel numbers are 3809 to 3815.

96th Regiment of Foot, 1841 to 1848, Australia; 1844 to 1846, New Zealand (detachment only)

The first division of the 96th Regiment reached Sydney on 22 September 1841 and after six days the men were marched to Windsor where they remained until June 1842. The Regimental Headquarters was then established at Parramatta. In January 1843 Headquarters was transferred to Launceston from whence it administered detachments located at twenty-two stations throughout Australia.

On 28 March 1844, under orders from Lieut General M. C O'Connell, a detachment under the command of Lieut Colone Hulme was despatched to New Zealand. Here it took part in the fighting at Kokorariki and at Stokes Pah; heavy casualties were sustaine in both operations. In 1847 the detachment returned to Launcesto and the following year the Regiment received orders to prepare fo service in India. The last division of the 96th left King George Sound, Western Australia, in January 1849.

In 1881 the 96th became the 2nd Battalion of the Manchester Regiment.

(Coleman, K. *A Short History of the Military Forces in New South Wales 1770-1900* Sydney: Victoria Barracks Museum Society, 1977.)

Locations of records of the 96th Regiment

Many of the officers' particulars of service would be found in the Hart's Army Lists and at the Public Record Officer under WO 25. The New Zealand War Medal Rolls would include the names of a number of officers who were in the 1844 and 1845 New Zealand operations.

Microfilm copies of the Pay and Muster Rolls of the 96th are in the National Libraries of Australia and New Zealand. The reel numbers for the years 1839 to 1849 are 3889 to 3896. For reasons unknown the names of members of the 96th do not appear on the New Zealand War Medal Roll.

99th (Lanarkshire Volunteers) Regiment of Foot, 1843 to 1856; 1845 to 1846 New Zealand, (detachment only)

The 99th underwent a number of changes in title but during its tour of duty in Australia and New Zealand it was the Lanarkshire Volunteers Regiment mainly recruited in the Glasgow area. It began leaving for Australia during 1842 by detachments, two of which were to suffer on the voyage. One sailed in the convict ship *Somersetshire* which arrived at the Cape of Good Hope in March 1842. A mixed party consisting of men of the 57th and 99th were guarding 215 prisoners and four of the 99th openly mutinied. A hastily convened court-martial at Cape Town sentenced the ringleader (Private John Agnew) to death by firing squad; two accomplices received life sentences, and a fourth turned Queen's Evidence. Several months later the convict ship *Waterloo* dropped anchor at Cape Town and on 27 June 1842 in a severe gale its chains snapped and the vessel began taking in water before breaking up. More than 100 convicts and fifteen men of the 99th were drowned in what became the worst shipwreck of the transportation era. In addition to the convicts and troops, four of the soldiers' wives and fourteen of their children also perished.

The 99th Regiment spent only a short time at Sydney before being moved to Van Diemen's Land and then returned to Sydney in August

1844. Officers and other ranks were posted to the Mounted Police and to the various outstations in Australia. In May 1845 two companies were ordered to New Zealand where they took part in the assault on Ohaiani Pah but were obliged to retire with heavy losses; four officers and fourteen men were killed and twenty-seven were wounded. On 10 January 1846 the detachment was present at the assault and capture of Ruapekapeka. During the same month a reinforcement of 105 men arrived from Sydney and the 99th Regiment took part in several more engagements with the rebel Maoris before returning to Australia in August 1847. The Regiment had been quartered at the old George Street Barracks in Sydney, the scene of a minor mutiny in December 1845. A strong force of the 11th Regiment had been dispatched from Hobart to restore order which resulted in the two Regiments exchanging their stations, although a small party of 99th men stayed on at the Sydney Barracks until the Regiment was posted to England in 1856.

During the disturbances on the Victorian goldfields in 1854 a force of the 99th Regiment was sent from Tasmania to Melbourne to stand by in case of further uprisings among the miners. The main body of the Regiment was later posted from Hobart to Melbourne where it remained until embarking for England in 1856; it had served continuously in the Australasian colonies for almost thirteen years.

In 1881 the 99th Regiment became the 2nd Battalion of the Wiltshire Regiment.

Locations of records of the 99th Regiment of Foot

Officers who served in the first Maori war are noted with the particulars of their war service in Hart's Army Lists. The Public Record Office holds officers' documents which may include biographical details. Pay and Muster Rolls for the years 1841 until 1857 are available in the National and State libraries of Australia and New Zealand. The reel numbers are 3896 to 3905.

The names of a number of men who served with the 99th do not appear on the New Zealand War Medal Roll.

11th (North Devonshire) Regiment of Foot, 1845 to 1857

The First Division of the 11th Regiment, which consisted of four companies, sailed from Chatham in the freight ship *Castle Eden* on 18 July 1845; the remaining companies left in the *Ramillies* on 5 August 1845.

The service of the 11th Regiment in Australia was divided between Hobart and Sydney and at the latter station a number of local citizens petitioned for its retention for a further tour of duty. Both officers and the rank and file acquired a reputation for being helpful and well behaved. They provided the city of Sydney with a fire brigade which distinguished itself by putting out large fires including the Ormond House disaster and the blaze which almost destroyed a well-known brewery. Fatigue parties detailed by the 11th contributed much to the laying out of Sydney Cricket Ground.

When the Regiment was ordered to prepare to return to England more than 100 of its members applied to take their discharge in Australia. The news of the massacre of European women and children at Cawnpore reached Sydney and many of these men re-engaged for further service. The 11th sailed for England on 23 October 1857.

In 1881 the 11th Regiment of Foot became the Devonshire Regiment.

Location of records of the 11th Regiment

The Public Record Office holds the service records of officers and the documents of soldiers who were discharged to a pension.

The microfilm copies of the Pay and Muster Rolls are available for the years 1845 to 1858 in the National and State libraries of Australia and New Zealand. The reel numbers are 3703 to 3714.

58th (Rutlandshire) Regiment of Foot, 1844 to 1845, 1846 to 1847, Australia; 1845 to 1858, New Zealand

The 58th Regiment was stationed at Sydney for a few months before becoming involved in the first Maori war in 1845. Late in 1846 it returned to Sydney where it remained until 1847 when it moved back to New Zealand to take part in the fighting around Wanganui. The 58th became a part of the garrison at New Plymouth. During the twelve years that the 58th Regiment was stationed in New Zealand a large number of its rank and file took their discharge and settled. Before leaving in 1858 the Commanding Officer of the Regiment presented its colours to the inhabitants of Auckland. Since 1933 these colours have been on display at the Auckland Institute and Museum. When the colours were formally handed over the ceremony was attended by nearly 400 descendants of men of the 58th and sixty descendants of Maori chiefs who had fought against them.

Locations of records of the 58th Regiment

Officers' war service is in Hart's Army Lists. Their personal documents and those of rank and file pensioners would be at the Public Record Office.

Microfilm of Pay and Muster Rolls of the 58th from 1843 to 1859 are available at the National and State libraries in Australia and New Zealand. The reel numbers are 3826 to 3837.

Some of the names of men of the 58th are missing from the New Zealand War Medal Roll.

65th (2nd Yorkshire, North Riding) Regiment of Foot, 1846 to 1849 detachments in Australia; 1846 to 1865 New Zealand

The 65th Regiment sailed to Australia in three transports, the *Java*, the *Samuel Boddington*, and the *Prestonjee Bomanjee*. Three smaller detachments sailed later during the latter part of 1845 and May 1846. The Regiment spent only a few months at Hobart before being transferred to New Zealand, leaving behind a rear party consisting of two officers and thirty-two rank and file.

The 65th Regiment took part in many engagements of the first and second Maori wars and during that time a mutual respect developed between its members and the Maori warriors. To them the Regiment was known as the 'Hickety Pips' because that was the nearest they could get to pronouncing 'Sixty-Fifth'.

The 65th served the longest tour of duty in New Zealand, having been stationed there for nineteen continuous years. When it finally departed for England in 1865 its ranks numbered only 370 NCOs and Privates; the remainder had taken their discharge and settled.

Locations of records of the 65th Regiment

Officer's war service could be in Hart's Army Lists and his personal documents would be at the Public Record Office. The service records of the rank and file would also be at the Public Record Office provided they were pensioners. Out-pensioners' records for those who settled in New Zealand have been microfilmed and are available in the same way as the Pay and Muster Rolls. Australian National and State libraries have copies of the latter but for New Zealand researchers those for the 65th Regiment only are held by the Auckland Public Library. The reel numbers, which cover the years 1845 to 1865, are 3841 to 3860.

12th (East Suffolk) Regiment of Foot, Australia, 1854 to 1860 New Zealand, 1860 to 1866

The 12th Regiment arrived in Australia in 1854 when there was th threat of war with Russia, and internal instability and social unrest on the Victorian goldfields. The men of the 12th Regiment were called upon on two occasions to aid the civil authority. The companies stationed at Melbourne were part of the force that attacked the stockade at Eureka. In 1858 a contingent consisting of 300 of the 12th, sixty sailors from HMS *Fawn,* and a strong force of Mounted Police marched to Lambing Flat, near Young, to subdue a riot which had broken out between the Chinese and European miners.

During the Regiment's tour of duty in Australia its personnel was thinly spread, in small detachments, over the Australian continent. From the latter part of 1860 men of the 12th began moving to New Zealand although a small party remained at Sydney until 1863. In New Zealand the Regiment formed a part of the garrison at New Plymouth and took a minor part in the Taranaki campaign of 1860 and 1861. It was also involved in a number of engagements during the second Maori war. The 12th Regiment returned to England in 1866.

Locations of records of the 12th Regiment

Officer's service in the Maori wars would be noted in Hart's Army Lists; other personal documents are at the Public Record Office. Only pensioned soldiers of the 12th would still be at this location and their records, as pensioners settled in New Zealand, are on microfilm. Copies of these are available at all National and State libraries in Australia and New Zealand as are the Pay and Muster Rolls. Reel numbers are 3714 to 3732 and run from the years 1854 to 1868.

77th (East Middlesex) Regiment of Foot, 1857 to 1858

While serving in Ireland in 1857 the 77th Regiment received orders to embark for Australia and on 1 June of that year its personnel sailed from Kingstown (Dun Laog haire). After a stormy voyage they landed at Sydney on 30 September 1857.

The Regiment's period of service in Australia was short, and early in 1858 it was ordered to prepare for a tour of duty in Hong Kong but because of the mutiny in India its destination was hurriedly changed. On 20 April 1858 the Headquarters of the 77th sailed for Calcutta in HMS *Megaera* and the remainder of the Regiment followed in the *Raby Castle* a few days later. It did not return to England until 1870.

In 1881 the 77th Regiment became the 2nd Battalion of the Middlesex Regiment.

Locations of the records of the 77th Regiment

The officers of the Regiment would have details of their war service well covered in the Hart's Army Lists. Many saw action during the Crimean War (1854-1856) although few, if any, were able to settle in Australia or New Zealand at the time their Regiment was with the Australian Command.

The Pay and Muster Rolls of the 77th for the years 1857 to 1859 are available on microfilm in the National and State libraries of Australia and New Zealand. The reel numbers are 3875 to 3877.

14th (Buckinghamshire) Regiment of Foot, 2nd Battalion New Zealand, 1859 to 1866; Australia, 1866 to 1870

The 2nd Battalion of the 14th Regiment was raised in 1858 and was posted to New Zealand a year later. It served in the Maori wars of 1860 to 1861 and 1863 to 1866, taking part in many engagements including Kuit Kara, Koheroa, Rangariri, and Waikato Pah.

Early in 1867 the Regiment was transferred to Australia with its headquarters at Melbourne. It did not serve in New South Wales but a detachment of five officers and 175 rank and file arrived at Sydney in March 1869. The visit was short and its purpose is not recorded.

According to the official history of the 14th Regiment its stay in the Australian colonies was largely for 'rest and recreation'. The writer commented on the colonists' kindness to the Regiment. Cricket matches, race meetings, and many other social and sporting events were organised for its benefit.

Under orders to return to England, the 14th Regiment embarked at Melbourne in the *Windsor Castle* on 19 March 1870.

In 1881 the 14th Regiment was re-designated the Prince of Wales Own West Yorkshire Regiment.

Locations of records of the 14th Regiment

Because of its long involvement in the Maori wars the officers who took part in the major engagements are recorded in the Hart's Army Lists. A number of these and a proportion of the rank and file may have settled in New Zealand.

The Pay and Muster Rolls of the 2nd/14th are available on microfilm at all the National and State libraries in Australia and New Zealand. These cover the years 1860 to 1870 and the reel numbers are 3734 to 3748.

Above, *British troops embarking for England on 23 August 1870. The last of the British soldiers to have served in Australia and New Zealand. The 18th (Royal Irish) Regiment and Royal Artillery, embarking in the* Royal Eagle

Right, *Forage cap badge of the 18th Royal Irish Regiment*

18th (Royal Irish) Regiment of Foot, 2nd Battalion New Zealand, 1863 to 1870; Australia, January 1870 to September 1870

The last British infantry regiment to be stationed in Australia or New Zealand was the 18th. It arrived in July 1863 to take part in the Maori wars and served in a number of major engagements from 1863 until 1866. Officers and men were popular with the New Zealand colonists but they were disliked by Maoris. A number of the infantry were known to have mistreated prisoners. Early in 1869 the 2nd/18th received orders to relieve the 50th which was stationed in Sydney. The European population strongly opposed the move and a number of letters appeared in the local press appealing to the Imperial Government to allow the Regiment to stay in New Zealand. The New Zealand Government tried to compromise and the Regiment's departure was delayed a few months. The decision had been made that colonial governments would be responsible for their own land defence. In January 1870 the Battalion Headquarters of the 2nd/18th Regiment and four companies were posted to Sydney and other companies and detachments were sent to the various Australian stations in the major centres of settlement.

The 'self reliant policy' as it applied to the Australasian colonies was promulgated on 14 August 1870 and almost immediately the 18th began preparations to embark for England. On 27 August the *Newcastle Morning Herald* reported details of the embarkation of the 18th from Circular Quay. The main body of the Regiment sailed, along with the last of the Royal Artillery, in the *Silver Eagle*; the rear party left Sydney on 6 September 1870.

More than 100 NCOs and Privates of the 18th applied for their discharge to settle in Australia. Thirty-seven deserted just before the Regiment embarked.

Locations of the records of the 18th Regiment

The service of officers who were in the Maori wars are detailed in Hart's Army Lists. A number of officers and rank and file would have settled in New Zealand and some may have served in militia and other local Armed Forces.

The Pay and Muster Rolls for the 2nd/18th Regiment have been microfilmed and are available for the years 1863 to 1870 in National and State libraries of Australia and New Zealand. The reel numbers are 3750 to 3758.

The 18th (Royal Irish) Regiment became the Royal Irish Regiment in 1881 but was disbanded, along with many other distinguished Irish regiments, when the Irish Free State was formed in 1922.

The suggested uniform (to be made by members' wives) of the NSW Volunteer Force in 1854. It was rejected in favour of a dark green tunic and trousers based on those worn by English rifle regiments

---O---

PART THREE

---O---

Australian military forces of the colonial period, 1800 to 1901 — the Australian Commonwealth Military Force — wars and campaigns — the records that are available in Australia

The colonial and post-colonial periods in Australia

The colonial period

Loyal Associations

The first locally raised military force in Australia was the Loyal Associations. Consisting of two companies, one was formed in Sydney and the other at Parramatta. It was first raised in 1800 and with a short period of inactivity between 1802 and 1804 it continued until its disbandonment in 1810. Members were drawn from all sections of society both bond and free; the officers were mainly medical men and the NCOs and Privates were business and professional men, artisans, and labourers. They were all unpaid but were issued with the uniforms of the New South Wales Corps. They met for drill and instruction on Saturday afternoons.

The First New South Wales Volunteer Force

From the dissolution of the Loyal Associations until the war scare of 1854 little thought was given to local citizen military forces in the Australian colonies.

In 1854 British and France were at war with Russia and the depleted Imperial garrison force was ill-equipped to defend the widely scattered settlements in Australia.

Following the pattern set up by Britain, the colonial governments formed small volunteer military forces. These were unpaid and in many cases were required to supply their own uniforms and arms. The officers and the rank and file members came mainly from the business and professional strata because tradesmen and labourers could not afford to be members of the rather exclusive organisation. After the armistice in 1856 interest in military matters waned and the Volunteer units broke up, although a few small groups continued to meet and drill unofficially.

Volunteer Forces, 1860

The close of 1859 saw the beginning of a generally unsettled period in the Pacific region. Russia had built a strong naval base at Vladivostok, the French were expanding their empire in the South Pacific, the Maoris were again rebelling, and North America was on the verge of civil war.

Interest in volunteer military forces was revived and the Australian colonial governments, particularly those of New South Wales and Victoria, authorised the formation of companies of artillery, cavalry, infantry, engineers, and naval brigades. On this occasion governments gave more material support; uniforms and equipment were provided although members were still unpaid unless they were called out for active duty.

Fears of war settled down once again but interest was maintained in some colonies by offering volunteers free land grants after a five-year period of efficient service.

First Permanent Forces

When the Imperial troops left Australia in 1870 the colonial governments were encouraged by Britain to adopt a 'self reliant policy' and be responsible for maintaining their own land defence forces. The Royal Navy was to provide sea defence.

In 1878 a system of 'partial payment' was introduced in the Volunteer Force of New South Wales in an attempt to improve efficiency. From 1877 until 1883 the Jervois–Scratchley Report on Australian defence was compiled. Among the many recommendations was the suggestion that not too much reliance should be placed on unpaid Volunteers. As a result of this Report, all the Australian colonies, with the exception of Western Australia, were recommended to provide a certain number of troops, both permanent and part-time, to be trained in specified branches of Army and naval defence.

Between 1883 and 1901 the colonial armies were built up from a total force of 9,423 to more than 29,000 by Federation when all the naval and military forces of the former Australian colonies amalga-

Sydney Volunteers, 1862. Members of the NSW team which contested the Inter-Colonial Rifle Shooting contest held in Melbourne. The team was shipwrecked off Green Cape on its way home to Sydney. The men survived, but their equipment and tropies were lost

ate of the Newcastle Company, NSW Rifle eers, c.1864. The silver stripe on the right eeve is for 12 months' efficiency in arms

A junior ensign of the NSW Volunteer Artillery, c.1865

mated. Australia's population at Federation, in 1901, was 3.8 million people. This amalgamation took place over a period of years from 1901. All colonies had formed a small permanent force; and with the exception of Western Australia and Tasmania all had adopted a militia and all had included members of rifle clubs in the general defence scheme.

Sudan Campaign

On 11 January 1885 news reached Sydney that General Gordon had been murdered in Khartoum. The New South Wales Government offered military aid to Britain and a contingent consisting of volunteers from New South Wales was sent to serve in the Sudan. This support consisted of an infantry battalion, a battery of artillery, and an ambulance section which left Sydney on 3 March 1885 and arrived at the Red Sea port of Suakin on 29 March. Here it was brigaded with the Guards Regiments but saw little action. Casualties were light with a few slightly wounded. However a number of men were left behind in hospital suffering with dysentery and malaria. The contingent returned home in June 1885 and were later awarded both the British Egyptian Campaign Medal with the 'Suakin' clasp and the Khedive Star given by the Egyptian Government.

China War (Boxer Rebellion)

In 1900 a group of Chinese, known as 'Boxers', rebelled against the presence of foreigners who occupied areas of their country for the purpose of safeguarding trading interests.

In June 1900 the premier of New South Wales received an appeal from the British Colonial Office suggesting that vessels of the Australian Naval Squadron should be sent to China to aid the Europeans. The New South Wales, South Australian and Victorian governments sent ships with a total of 656 men but most of the military action was carried out by German troops. The Australians returned home on 25 April 1901.

Commonwealth military forces

The Constitution Act empowered the Australian Commonwealth to legislate for the naval and military defence of the six constituent States as well as for the Commonwealth as a whole. The transfer of the State armed forces to the Commonwealth was legally carried out in March

Right, *Captain R. Scobie (standing) and Major G. J. Burnage of the 2nd NSW Mounted Infantry, 1901*
Below, a detachment of NSW Lancers preparing to take part in the procession in London to mark Queen Victoria's Diamond Jubilee in 1897

1901 when the responsibility for defence passed to the Defence Department, one of the seven departments of the Executive Council.

The task of combining the six colonial armies was carried out by Major-General Sir Edward Hutton and during 1903 and 1904 the Defence Force Act created the legislative basis for the Australian military system. Titles of regiments and other formations were changed to 'Australian' in place of the former State prefix while the numerical titles were usually changed also.

The Kitchener Report, issued in 1901, recommended that the Commonwealth should be divided into military areas with each one providing a definite proportion of fighting units. Compulsory military training was introduced in 1911. Men were liable to be retained for military training until the age of twenty-six and arrangements were made to train 200 NCOs as instructors for the new Army.

The Royal Military College at Duntroon, near Canberra, was opened in June 1911 to train cadet officers; the course was of four years' duration followed by one year in England, India, Hong Kong or Singapore.

Boer War

Between 1899 and 1902 the Australian colonies and the Commonwealth sent a total of 848 officers and 13,327 men to South Africa to fight in the Anglo-Boer War. The dead numbered 120 officers and 1,280 men of lower ranks; the majority of the deaths were from enteric fever.

Six Victoria Crosses were awarded to Australian soldiers.

World War I

On 4 August 1914 (5 August Australian time) following the invasion of Belgium, Britain went to war against Germany. As the British Empire was constituted at that time the dominions and colonies were automatically involved. In Australia General W. T. Bridges was commissioned to organise a force for service overseas which he named the Australian Imperial Force, a title that was to continue in World War II.

Of the first 20,000 troops sent overseas, most of the officers had served in the militia and about one-third of the rank and file had previous militia service. Little more than one-quarter of all ranks were British-born. During the hostilities (which ceased on 11 November 1918) the Australian armed forces served in theatres of war on three continents. A total of 416,834 men had enlisted for military service; 330,000 had served overseas and 52,258 were either killed or listed missing. There were 4.5 million Australians at census in 1911.

Re-organisation between the wars

At the close of World War I it was decided to change the numbers of units and formations of citizens forces (made up of Militia and Volunteers) to correspond with those of the Australian Imperial Forces (AIF). This was to maintain some of the traditions that had been established in times of war.

In 1921 the Commonwealth Government took measures to restrict compulsory training. At this time the control of rifle clubs passed from military to civilian administration.

During 1922 and 1923 drastic cuts were made in the strength of the Australian Military Forces and the period of training for the citizens forces was reduced to two years.

Compulsory training was phased out in 1929 and from 1 January 1930 enlistment was voluntary and the citizen force was re-designated the militia.

World War II

At the outbreak of World War II on 3 September 1939 the Australian Army stood at 2,800 officers and men in the permanent force backed by a militia of 80,000. In November 1939 the Commonwealth Government re-introduced compulsory military training. At 1939 the non-Aboriginal population in Australia was 7 million.

Between 1940 and 1945 Australian forces were engaged in theatres of war in Europe, the Middle East, Greece, Malaya, and many parts of the West Pacific. They also served with the Allied Occupation Force in Japan. At the end of World War II the strength of the Australian Army was 358,000 men and 22,700 women.

Casualties in operations against Germany and Italy were 3,631 dead and against Japan, 17,505 dead.

The total enlistment in Australia during World War II was 691,400 men and 35,800 women representing about one-eightieth of the population.

Korean War

On 25 June 1950 the North Korean Army crossed the 38th parallel beginning a three-year involvement in which some twenty member-countries of the United Nations served.

St.[1225

OATH OF ENGAGEMENT.

I, *John Maddison* swear that I will well and truly

serve our Sovereign Lady the Queen, in the *New South Wales Infantry*
or two years if required

for the term of *One* years, or until sooner lawfully discharged, dismissed,

or removed; and that I will resist Her Majesty's enemies, and cause Her Majesty's

peace to be kept both on land and at sea, and that I will in all matters appertaining

to my Service, faithfully discharge my duty according to law.

SO HELP ME GOD.

_____ *John Maddison* Signature of Recruit.

_____ { Signature of   manding or other
Capt.   { Commissio   Officer before whom
          { the Oath }   -een taken.

Date *10 . 2 - 85*

Private John Maddison's Attestation Papers for the Sudan War, 1885

...me and Number	John Maslderon
... ...	26
...ur of { Eyes	Blue
Hair	Light
Complexion	Fair
...ht...	5 . 9½
...s	No
...e or calling	Miner
...ion	Eng.
...ied or single	Single
...try	Victoria

NEW SOUTH WALES MILITARY FORCE.

QUESTIONS TO BE PUT TO THE RECRUIT ON ENGAGING.

St. 1224

1. What is your name?	John Madolism
2. In what parish, and in or near what town, and in what county, were you born?	Smythes Dale Vic
3. What is your age?	26
4. What is your trade or calling?	Miner
5. Are you an apprentice?	No
6. Are you married; if so, state number of children under 14 years of age?	Single
7. Are you ruptured or lame; have you been subject to fits; or have you any disability or disorder which impedes the free use of your limbs or unfits you for ordinary labour?	No
8. Are you willing to be engaged to serve in the Military Force of New South Wales?	Yes
9. Have you ever served in the Army, Marines, Ordnance, or Navy?	No
10. Have you ever been rejected as unfit for Her Majesty's Service?	No
11. What is your height?	5 · 9 ½

Australia sent nine ships of the Royal Australian Navy, a Fighter Squadron of the Royal Australian Air Force, the 1st, 2nd and 3rd Battalions of the Royal Australian Regiment.

When the armistice was signed on 27 July 1953 casualties in the United Nations forces totalled 73,500 dead, of which 1,538 were Australian.

Australia's population was 8 million in 1950.

The Vietnam conflict

Australian Armed Forces became involved in Vietnam under the terms of the SEATO Alliance. In July 1962 the Australian Government sent thirty officers and other ranks to South Vietnam to assist in Army training; two years' later a further forty were sent along with six RAAF aircraft and crews. By 1968 Australia's population was 12 million.

By the end of 1972, when the Australian forces were being withdrawn, there had been more than 53,000 Australian men engaged in the conflict; many of whom were conscripts. Among the casualties were about 450 dead and some 2,540 wounded. Four Victoria Crosses were awarded to Australian service men, two posthumously.

Malayan Emergency and Indonesian Confrontation (*Konfrontasi*)

Although not a declared war, a number of Australian Naval, Army and Air Force personnel were involved in Malaysia in combatting guerrilla insurgency between 1955 and 1966. In Indonesia, undergoing political restructuring, SEATO forces were engaged in peace keeping duties.

Locations of Australian Army records

Colonial period

Official records for the colonial period in Australia are sparse. Possibly lack of centralised control around the time of Federation could have led to the loss of many records of that period. However, it is possible to gather fragments of biographical information in Parliamentary Papers such as *Votes & Proceedings* of colonial governments; Government *Gazettes* for appointments to commissioned ranks in the Volunteer and Permanent Forces; and Returns of the Colonies for names of officers. The Commonwealth Archives Office holds correspondence files, Muster Rolls, Pay Rolls and so on for the Victoria Force for 1863 to 1911.

The Australian War Memorial holds volumes which contain the New South Wales Marriage Register for the years 1888 to 1911, and a Marriage and Baptism Register for 1876 to 1890.

Sudan Campaign
The State Archives Office of New South Wales has a collection of correspondence dealing with this campaign and the Australian War Memorial holds a number of Attestation Papers of Commonwealth volunteers.

South African (Boer War)
The Archives Office in Canberra holds copies of Discharge Books of men who served in this war, and also a selection of documents, such as applications to enter South Africa, nominal rolls of units, and unit states which give details of the strength of a unit showing the number of officers, NCOs, including the sick, those on leave, deserted, or dead.

Locations

CRS B168, MP 307, MP 488/7, MP 729/1, and MP 744
CP 601/2
Commonwealth Archives Office SP 820/1.
     State Archives Offices also hold some records of men from their own States.

References and resources

For research on members of the Australian Armed Forces of the colonial, and Commonwealth periods.

Australian Dictionaries of Biography   Since the end of the 19th century four volumes have been compiled with various Series Editors. A number of military men are featured in the dictionaries, especially in the earlier works. The *Dictionary of Australasian Biography* London: Hutchinson, 1892 was compiled by P. Mennell, see also Dornbusch *Australian Military Biography* 1963; publisher unknown, and Gibbney and Burns *A Biographer's Index of Parliamentary Returns for New South Wales, Queensland and Victoria 1850 to 1889.*
Early editions of directories and almanacs will often give the names of officers, and sometimes NCOs of the local military forces under the head 'Military Establishment'.
Australian Military Forces   The personal documents of all members are held at the Central Army Records Office in Melbourne.

Discharge Certificate, 1st Australian Imperial Expeditionary Force issued to Private J. S. Neely in December 1919. The Certificate shows date of enlistment, age and place of birth, length of service and date of discharge. It also gives a physical description of the soldier and his age on discharge

Australian War Memorial Library holds a collection of Army Records which deal mainly with World Wars I and II, such as AIF Nominal Rolls, AIF Embarkation Rolls, and Nominal Rolls of Deceased. It also has a number of war diaries, troopship lists and records, and some Red Cross correspondence. The earlier holdings include some enlistment papers for the Sudan War.

Australian Aboriginal participation

Australian Aborigines and Torres Straits Islanders have taken part in every major conflict after the Maori wars that has involved white Australians. Although official records do not differentiate between the races, there have been a number of interested persons who have compiled lists of members of these races who have served in the Australian Armed Forces. The campaigns covered include World Wars I and II, Korea, Malaya, and Vietnam. Much of the research was carried out by Mr Don Cameron, the Queensland parliamentarian, and his original material and sources may be found at the Research Section of the Australian War Memorial. Major Robert A. Hall, a military historian, has also done much work in this area and has concentrated mainly on World War II. He has located the particulars of about 830 Torres Straits Islanders and more than 700 Australian mainland Aborigines who served in this war. Other interested persons include Mr David Huggins of the Aboriginal Development Commission, and Miss Rita Bostock of the Queensland Department of Education.

To date very little information has been published on the Aborigines' role in European warfare.

PART FOUR

New Zealand military forces of the colonial and Dominion periods — wars and campaigns — locations of the records in New Zealand

British regiments and corps stationed in New Zealand

80th (Staffordshire) Regiment of Foot (Detachment)	1840-1844
96th Regiment of Foot (Detachment)	1843-1845
99th (Lanarkshire) Regiment of Foot	1845-1847
58th (Rutlandshire) Regiment of Foot*	1845-1858
65th (Yorkshire) Regiment of Foot	1846-1865
40th (2nd Somersetshire) Regiment of Foot	1860-1866
57th (West Middlesex) Regiment of Foot	1860-1866
14th (Buckinghamshire) 2nd Battalion	1860-1867
12th (East Suffolk) Regiment of Foot	1860-1866
70th (Surrey) Regiment of Foot	1863-1866
43rd (Monmouthshire) Light Infantry	1863-1866
50th (Queen's Own) Regiment of Foot	1863-1866
18th (Royal Irish) Regiment of Foot 2nd Battalion	1863-1870
68th (Durham) Light Infantry	1864-1866
Royal Artillery	1846-1870
Royal Engineers	1840-1870
Royal Corps of Sappers and Miners	1840-1857
Army Hospital Corps	1861-1870
Commissariat Staff Corps	1861-1870
Commissariat Transport Corps (Detachment)	1861-1866
Military Train and Horse Transport	1864-1867

---

* The 58th Regiment of Foot saw divided duty between Australia and New Zealand.

The colonial and Dominion periods in New Zealand

New Zealand Militia

A Government Ordnance of 1845 enabled Militia units to be raised for temporary service in their own districts during times of emergency. The system had ceased by 1868 except in a few areas where unrest persisted. In the latter years the role formerly filled by Militia was carried out by the Corps of Volunteers.

Permanent Militia

The Permanent Militia was established in 1886 to take over the military duties of the Armed Constabulary. In 1909 it was redesignated the Permanent Force.

Volunteer Corps

Although the Volunteer Corps was not officially recognised until an Act of 1865, it had been flourishing for some years and had been employed, unofficially, during the early New Zealand wars. Volunteer Corps remained an integral part of the New Zealand Defence Force until it was superseded by the Territorial Army during 1910 and 1911. Each Corps was local in character and remained self-contained except for periodic inspections and observance of weapon-training regulations.

Colonial Defence Force

This branch of the Armed Forces was organised on a provincial basis

Waist-belt plate, New Zealand Militia

Officer's pouch, New Zealand Volunteer Force, 1872–1898

but came under the supervision of the General Assembly. It ceased to exist in 1867 and many of its members transferred to the Armed Constabulary.

The Maori wars

The Maori wars were a series of campaigns fought by Imperial and colonial troops between 1844 and 1872 against various combinations of Maori tribes. The fighting was confined mainly to the North Island of New Zealand and the primary cause was the question of land ownership. The first serious outbreak occurred in 1844 and companies of the 96th and 99th Regiments were posted from Australia.

After a period of comparative peace trouble broke out again in 1859, this time in Taranaki. This is known as the second Maori war. The third Maori war began in 1863 in the Waikato region and in 1864 there was more serious fighting in the Tauranga area. In 1868 there was another Maori uprising, this time led by Te Kooti, when there was a massacre of Europeans at Poverty Bay. Soon afterwards a strange sect, the Ringatu, was involved in more serious trouble. At the peak of the hostilities there were almost 20,000 troops involved, 10,000 regulars, more than 9,000 local European volunteers, Militia, and hundreds of loyal Maoris. More than 2,500 men went from Australia, many with their wives and children, to serve with the Waikato Militia. During the wars 560 British and New Zealand servicemen and 250 loyalist Maoris died. It is believed that the rebel side lost 2,500 killed.

An element of mutual respect existed between the British soldiers and the Maori warriors as both shared a common contempt for the local politicians and land speculators. When the men of the 65th Regiment left New Zealand in 1866 having fought the rebel Maoris for almost twenty years, they erected a unique monument to their former foes. In St John's Anglican Church at Awamutu is a tablet installed by the 65th, dedicated to the Maori dead. It is inscribed with the text, 'I say unto you, love your enemies'.

British forces in New Zealand, 1840 to 1870

Towards the end of the 1830s the ever-increasing European population called for some measure of protection, and a small detachment of British troops was sent to New Zealand from Australia. By April 1840 a company of the 80th Regiment was well established in and around Auckland. A party of men from the Regiment was present at the Treaty of Waitangi. The 80th Regiment was not involved in the Maori wars and thus not entitled to the New Zealand War Medal.

The role played by the British troops in New Zealand differed considerably from that in Australia. There were no transported convicts to guard, no remote outstations, no extremes of climate, no long periods of dull peacetime routine, and very few quasi-civilian duties. There was, however, plenty of action with ample opportunity to display military prowess. In New Zealand there was more involvement with the locally raised Armed Forces, whether Armed Constabulary, Militia or volunteers.

Between 1840 and 1870 fourteen British infantry regiments, the usual support troops, and detachments of Royal Naval personnel saw service in New Zealand. At the completion of their service many officers and rank and file stayed in New Zealand and joined the local Armed Forces; many more settled as civilians.

43rd (Monmouthshire) Light Infantry Regiment, 1863 to 1866

The 43rd Regiment had been serving overseas continuously before being ordered to New Zealand. It sailed from India in the *Lady Jocelyn*, which called at Mauritius to pick up ballast, and arrived at Auckland on 11 December 1863. On the voyage many were sick, mainly through gastro-intestinal disorders, and fifty men were admitted to hospital. The rest marched to the camp at Otahuhu. Its total strength was about 600.

The Regiment was employed mainly on redoubt (fieldwork) duty on the Great South Road and in 1864 a large part of it was moved to the Bay of Plenty. About 300 of the 43rd took part in the debacle at Gate Pah but were able to regain their reputation at Te Ranga on 21 June 1864. The Regiment was moved to the Taranaki district before embarkation in March 1866 for England; by then it had been on foreign service for more than fifteen years.

In 1881 the 43rd Regiment became the 1st Battalion of the Oxfordshire and Buckinghamshire Light Infantry.

Locations of records of the 43rd Light Infantry

Officers' war service is recorded in the Hart's Army Lists; their statements of service may be at the Public Record Office. Many officers who were serving with the 43rd in New Zealand were still serving in 1871 when a register was completed with Application Certificates when the Purchase System was being wound up. These can be found

Forage cap badge (left) and coat button, 43rd (Monmouthshire) Light Infantry

Captain H. E. W. Preston of the 50th (Queen's Own) Regiment. He served with his regiment in Australia and New Zealand between 1860 and 1869, and settled in Sydney c.1870 where he died in 1905

under WO 74 at the Public Record Office. Before the Regiment left New Zealand about eighty NCOs and Privates took their discharge to settle in New Zealand or were transferred to the Commissariat or Hospital Corps. This allowed them to remain for a further three years or more.

The Pay and Muster Rolls are available for the years 1863 to 1866 at all Australasian National and State libraries. The reel numbers are 3792 to 3795.

70th (Surrey) Regiment of Foot, 1863 to 1866

The 70th Regiment arrived in New Zealand in 1863 and within a short time was engaged in a number of skirmishes in the Waikato district. In the major actions at Waiari, Te Awamutu, Orakau, and at Rangiaohia, the Regiment suffered a number of casualties.

The Regiment left in 1866, leading the general withdrawal of Imperial troops from New Zealand.

In 1881 the 70th Regiment became the 2nd Battalion of the East Surrey Regiment.

Locations of records of the 70th Regiment

Officers' records would be fairly complete at the Public Record Office as would those of rank and file members who were in receipt of a pension.

The Pay and Muster Rolls of the 70th Regiment are available for the years 1861 to 1865 at all Australasian National and State libraries; the reel numbers are 3863 to 3868.

68th (Durham Light Infantry) Regiment, 1864 to 1866

The 68th Regiment had been serving in Burma before arriving in New Zealand in 1864. Between 1864 and 1866 the Regiment was involved in many battles and skirmishes including Te Ranga, Te Papa, and Tauranga. A number of officers, NCOs and privates received awards for gallantry during these engagements.

The 68th Regiment left New Zealand in 1866.

In 1881 the 68th Regiment became the 1st Battalion of the Durham Light Infantry.

Locations of records of the 68th Regiment

The officers' records, like those of officers of the 43rd and 70th, would

A group of NCOs and Privates of the 68th Light Infantry in New Zealand, 1865. The sergeant at the far right is Sgt Murray, VC

be fairly complete at the Public Record Office. Hart's Army Lists includes notes on their war service.

The Pay and Muster Rolls for the 68th Regiment are available on microfilm for the years 1863 to 1866 and at all National and State libraries in Australia and New Zealand. The reel numbers are 3860 to 3862.

Army Medical Services: Army Hospital Corps, New Zealand 1861 to 1870

Medical services for British troops in Australia were provided by regimental surgeons and members of the colonial medical staff. Army hospitals were organised on a regimental basis and these were supervised by the regimental surgeon, or his assistant, with a hospital sergeant who was usually responsible for compounding the medicines and directing the regimental hospital orderlies.

The appalling conditions suffered by the sick and wounded during the Crimean War drew public attention to the lack of trained hospital personnel and the total absence of a co-ordinated system of military hospital administration. As a result of many public inquiries an Army Hospital Corps was formed from a class of recruit considered suitable for such duties. Men were trained in ambulance and nursing methods and a 'purveyor's department' trained men as cooks and storemen to man the new military hospitals. At this stage female nurses were not a part of the military hospital establishment. Regimental medical officers continued to be officers of the corps to which they were appointed, and hospital and medical administration came within the jurisdiction of the Army Medical Department.

In 1884 the Army Hospital Corps became the Medical Staff Corps and in 1898 all hospital and medical organisations were amalgamated to become the Royal Army Medical Corps.

The campaigns in New Zealand saw the end of the regimental system of hospital administration and the introduction of many innovations in the field of health care for the soldiers. Between 1861 and 1870 British military hospitals were established at Auckland, New Plymouth, Napier, and Wanganui.

Commissariat Staff Corps and 4th Battalion Military Train and Horse Transport, New Zealand, 1861 to 1870

Like the medical services, the Commissariat Department came under public scrutiny after the Crimean War. There was a need for an organised transport system and improvement in the way essential supplies were provided for the Army at war.

What had formerly been a quasi-civilian body came under military administration in 1859 with the formation of the Commissariat Staff Corps; the Military Train (of horses and carts) had been formed in 1856. The two Corps were re-titled frequently until 1888 when they were amalgamated to become the Army Service Corps.

Detachments of Commissariat Corps served with the combatant forces in New Zealand between 1861 and 1870. The 4th Battalion of the Military Train and Horse Transport which arrived at Auckland in February 1864, remained until 1867.

Royal New Zealand Fencibles, 1848 to 1853

In 1848 Governor Grey asked the British Government for a force of at least 2,500 soldiers to be stationed in New Zealand but, ever watchful on matters of expenditure, the authorities sent a corps of 500 Army pensioners.

Known as the Royal New Zealand Fencibles these old soldiers were expected to carry out certain military duties in return for free transport to New Zealand for their wives, families and themselves. They were given a cottage with an acre (0.4 ha.) of land which became their property after seven years.

Ten ships brought the Fencibles to New Zealand: the *Ann*, the *Berhampore, Berwick Castle, Clifton, Inchinnan, Minerva, Oriental Queen, Ramillies, Sir George Seymour*, and the *Sir Robert Sale*. These part-time troops were settled in villages at Howick, Panmure, and Onehunga during the period 1847 to 1853 to form a chain of defence posts across the isthmus to protect Auckland from Maori attack. In addition to their duties as a defence force the veterans were required to muster every Sunday at a church parade and to attend twelve day drills a year without pay.

Special Units Von Tempsky's Company of Forest Rangers, Captain Jackson's Company of Forest Rangers

These units were employed as scouts and bush fighters and saw a good deal of action fighting alongside and in front of regular and militia troops. Ideally suited to bush fighting, they were particularly useful in dealing with Maori war parties.

Waikato Militia, 1863 to 1866

Four regiments of Waikato Militia were raised between 1863 and 1866 and the majority of the recruits enlisted in New South Wales, Tasmania, and Victoria. These corps were intended as a military settlement scheme to maintain order in the Bay of Plenty and Waikato areas. Each man was to receive land in return for his services.

Many recruits came from the goldfields of Victoria and Otago and those disappointed in their search for gold were attracted to the prospect of free land. Much of the land surveyed for this purpose was unsuitable for farming and in time many allotments were either deserted or bought up by speculators.

A total of 1,784 Waikato Militiamen enrolled in Australia and a further thirty-one Australian volunteers enrolled in New Zealand. A high proportion of all volunteers would have been born in Britain or Ireland.

In spite of its militia status, the Waikato Militia fought with regiments of the Colonial Defence Force and several regular British Regiments during the third Maori War. Almost all members received the New Zealand War Medal of 1861-1866.

Locations of records of the Waikato Militia

The Army Department Archives at Wellington contain roll books of all four regiments. These give the members' names, places of birth, physical descriptions, occupations, marital status, and the names of the ships which conveyed the men to Auckland. Also there are the particulars of the land granted. The National Archives Office holds microfilm copies of the index of applications for land grants.

Military settlers, Taranaki and Hawkes Bay, 1863 to 1869

In addition to the Waikato Militia other military settlement schemes were tried, notably at Taranaki and Hawkes Bay. The Army Department Archives hold nominal rolls of settlers in these areas and each gives the dates of enlistment and particulars of the land grants. The Taranaki roll gives personal details and the names of the ships in which the recruits were conveyed to New Plymouth.

After the outbreak of hostilities in 1860, families were evacuated from Taranaki to Nelson. Information about these people may be found in both the Taranaki and Nelson Provincial Archives, as well as on microfilm at the Taranaki Museum, New Plymouth.

The actual service of military settlers, including those of the Waikato Militia, would frequently have been performed by a substitute, arranged by mutual agreement.

Armed Constabulary, 1867 to 1886

The duties performed by police in New Zealand differed from those in Australia in many respects, and the special needs of the European population were met by raising the Armed Constabulary in 1867. It had a dual military/police role and also undertook some public works. Members of this force saw active service from 1868 to 1871 and again at Parihaka in 1881. In 1886 its functions were divided between a fulltime coast defence corps and the police department.

The New Zealand Medal

The New Zealand Medal was issued to both Imperial and colonial troops who had served in the Maori wars between 1845 and 1847 and 1860 and 1866. The obverse side of the medal bears the head of Queen Victoria; the reverse side a laurel wreath. Medals were both dated and undated; the ribbon was royal blue with a red central stripe.

Although the Imperial and colonial issues of the medal were basically the same, the recipients were subject to a different set of conditions; broadly speaking, any man who had served in New Zealand with a British unit during the times of war was eligible for the medal. Members of the colonial forces were required to show that they had served in a military operation under fire. Members of the colonial forces who were seconded to British Army units such as the Commissariat Transport or Staff Corps were eligible for the Imperial issue. Regulations were in force in an attempt to avoid both medals being issued to the same man but it is known that a few colonial troops did get a double issue.

The New Zealand National Archives Office in Wellington holds a large number of records relating to the New Zealand Medal. This includes 4,500 application files for the colonial issue. This Office also holds microfilm records of the medals that were issued to British troops. However, these do not include parts of the 58th, 96th, and 99th regiments.

The last application for the medal was received as late as 1930; it was from James Thompson a former corporal of the 3rd Waikato Regiment.

Head dress badges, New Zealand Armed Constabulary. The badge on the left is the first pattern, which was in use till 1881. The badge worn after 1881 is on the right

Taranaki Militia pouch badge

Foreign Wars

The Boer War

Between October 1899 and April 1902 almost 6,500 men from New Zealand went to the war in South Africa, where two medals were awarded to Australian soldiers. The Queen's South African Medal, with clasps for a particular campaign, and the King's South African Medal and clasps awarded for 1901, 1902 or both.

World War I

Between 1914 and 1918 almost 100,000 New Zealand service men and women served in campaigns overseas. More than half of this number became casualties.

In 1916 conscription ballots were introduced in Australasia under the Military Service Act.

The British Government awarded two medals to New Zealand personnel who served overseas: the British War Medal and the Victory Medal. A special medal was awarded to those who served with the Mercantile Marine in dangerous waters.

The 'Turkish War'

Following the Chanak incident in 1922, the British Government requested help from New Zealand, but as there was no war, no troops were sent. Many serving members of the Armed Forces volunteered to go along with a number of exservice men and women.

World War II

Between September 1939 and August 1945 New Zealand servicemen and women served in every major campaign in the war against the Axis powers.

By July 1942 New Zealand had Armed Forces totalling 154,549 (not including the Auxiliary Patrol Service and Home Guard) and by April 1943 there were 124,194 men in the Home Guard. The number of seamen on the ships on the New Zealand Register in 1940 was 2,990. Of the total Armed Forces the women's services contributed 8,500.

As in World War I the numbers that were mobilised were large in proportion to the population but, fortunately, the casualty figures were lower. For the Navy, Army, Air Force, and Mercantile Marine the death toll was 11,625; 15,749 were wounded, and forty-six were missing.

Occupation of Japan known as 'J Force'

The 'J Force' reached Kure on 29 March 1946 and was quartered in and around Yamaguchi with detachments along the coast. The Royal New Zealand Air Force (RNZAF) was represented by No. 14 Fighter Squadron and elements of it remained in Japan until 'J Force' was withdrawn in September 1948.

Korean War known as 'K Force'

In July 1950 the Royal New Zealand Navy sent three frigates to serve in Korean waters and by March 1954 they had completed eight tours of duty. They intercepted pirate attacks on shipping, helped to beat off invasion attempts, made commando-type landings, and patrolled offshore.

Army volunteers were called for in July 1950 and by the end of August 1,100 had entered training camps. 'K Force' sailed for Korea in December 1950 and consisted of a Field Regiment of Artillery, a Signal Troop, a Field Maintenance Workshop, a Transport Platoon and a Reinforcement Training Unit.

The New Zealand gunners saw almost two-and-a-half-years of continuous action and were withdrawn in October 1954. 'K Force' returned home early in 1955 having lost thirty-seven killed, eighty wounded, and one man taken prisoner; he was subsequently returned at Panmunjom.

Malayan Emergency

This was a difficult campaign fought against Communist guerillas in dense jungle. New Zealand contributed elements of all its Armed Forces: a cruiser or frigate stationed at Singapore (still a part of Malaya), a Bomber Squadron of the Royal New Zealand Air Force, later replaced by a Fighter Squadron, and a Special Air Service unit to carry out parachute and commando-type operations with the Commonwealth Force. This was later replaced by a full infantry battalion. During the Malayan Emergency the New Zealand Army losses were ten men dead, and twenty-one wounded.

The Vietnam conflict

In June 1964 the New Zealand Government sent a non-combatant team of engineers and a medical contingent to Vietnam. The following year, in accordance with the terms of the SEATO Defence Alliance, a combatant force consisting of a battery of artillery was also sent. Over the next four years this force was gradually enlarged and in 1968 there were about 550 New Zealanders serving in the Vietnam conflict.

By the early 1970s significant opposition to New Zealand's participation in the conflict had grown and following the election of the Labor parties in Australia and New Zealand both Government withdrew their Armed Forces. By the end of 1972 the last of the New Zealand troops had left Vietnam. The New Zealand casualties suffered in that campaign were thirty-five dead, and 187 wounded.

Maori participation

Maoris have a long warrior tradition which dates back, at least, to their settlement in New Zealand between the 14th and 16th centuries. During that time they defeated and drove out the former inhabitants, the more passive Moriori people. Inter-tribal conflicts continued until they were pacified by European intervention towards the end of the 19th century. Maoris adapted well to the European form of warfare and from the 1880s were to participate in all foreign wars where New Zealand troops were involved.

Anglo-Boer War

During this war it was British Government policy not to involve the Maori people, but many served with the New Zealand Army by Anglicising their names.

World War I

When the ballot system was introduced by the Military Service Act of 1916 the Maoris were not required to register. With their declining population they were not encouraged to serve, but a total of 2,000 men volunteered for overseas service with the 1st NZEF (New Zealand Expeditionary Force). After Gallipoli a Maori Pioneer Battalion was formed and an all-Maori unit known as Te Hoko Whitu Atu fought on the Western Front in France. The last all-Maori unit to be formed was the 28th Battalion. In addition to Maoris a total of 458 Cook Islanders also served with the New Zealand Armed Forces.

World War II

The Maori population almost doubled during the inter-war years and this was reflected in the number that served in this war. Of Maoris enlisted, 5,300 were accepted for overseas service between 1939 and 1945. Of these some 3,000 fought with the Maori Battalion of the 2nd NZEF. They also served with Pakeha (white) units of all Armed Forces. Casualty figures were dead 612, wounded 1,906, missing eighteen, and prisoners-of-war 184. One Maori officer was awarded the Victoria Cross and ninety-seven others received Imperial awards. More detailed information may be obtained from The Librarian, Ministry of Defence, Private Bag, Wellington, New Zealand.

Locations of Service Records in New Zealand

Royal New Zealand Fencibles

In the War Office Records under WO 43 at the Public Record Office, London, a register gives the pensioner's pre-emption selection of the land allotment. This has been indexed and microfilmed and is available at the New Zealand National Archives. The original volumes are at the Auckland Branch of National Archives. The Wellington Branch has typescript copies of the passenger lists of the ten ships that conveyed the pensioners and their families to New Zealand. The originals of these are at the Public Record Office in London.

Special units

Von Tempsky's Forest Rangers and Captain Jackson's Forest Rangers
The Army Department holds records of No. 1 and No. 2 companies for the years 1863 to 1867 under AD 23/3. These are not indexed.

New Zealand Militia

A few fragments of these records are held by the New Zealand National Archives, particularly the rolls for Auckland, Wellington, and New Plymouth for the years 1843 to 1850, and for Marlborough and Nelson for 1864.

The detail varies as some only give the man's name, place of residence, and occupation. Others may give such details as age, or marital status.

Permanent Militia or Permanent Force

Roll books for the years 1886 to 1913 are held by National Archives. Only a few fragments of personal files have survived for the same period and these consist of surnames beginning with 'K' and 'L'. These are Reattestation Papers arranged alphabetically. There are also registers and a card index of commissions.

Volunteer Corps

Capitation rolls, which are lists of those attending drills, were sent in to the Government to qualify for funding. These exist for many corps from the 1860s to 1911. There are also Acquittance Rolls which list those who have been paid, with their signatures.

The New Zealand National Archives also holds personnel files of officers of Volunteer Corps for around 1903 to 1907, and lists of commissions between the years 1862 and 1911. A card index has been compiled which includes the corps that have been identified and shows whether the Capitation Rolls or other records survive at National Archives for each corps.

National Archives is planning a card index for individual Volunteers.

At present locating an individual Volunteer requires a knowledge of the corps in which he served. Clues to this may be found in the New Zealand War Medal index. Another possible source is the index to the naval and military settlers and the Volunteer Land Claims Commission.

Armed Constabulary

The New Zealand National Archives holds registers of service in the Armed Constabulary for the period 1867 to 1886. These give personal details along with details of enrolment and service. These records are now on microfilm in series Z. A nominal return of officers serving in July 1872 are in the Appendixes of the *Journals of the House of Representatives* under *AJHR* (H24-a).

Army commissions

A number of registers of Army commissions granted to officers of various corps, from 1859 to 1930, are held by the New Zealand National Archives. These registers usually give name, rank, dates of promotion, resignation, and so on, and sometimes a reference to a *Gazette* notice or to a relevant departmental file.

Rifle clubs

Files relating to rifle clubs throughout New Zealand were kept by the Army Department Archives until their administration passed to the National Rifle Association.

The Boer War

The records held by the New Zealand National Archives enable a fairly detailed picture to be built up on a man's service in this war.

The *AJHR* 1900-1902 (H6) contains printed nominal Rolls of the ten contingents and a Roll of Casualties. Other information includes the man's name, number, embarkation details, civilian occupation, and next of kin.

Personnel files for New Zealand soldiers who served in the Boer War are held at Base Records, Ministry of Defence, Wellington.

Medal Rolls are kept in the Army Department Archives. These are arranged by contingent and then alphabetically within rank. There is also a card index from which it is possible to find to which contingent an individual belonged. The New Zealand National Archives also holds files which relate to the issue of medals, officers' reports, diaries and rolls concerning New Zealand's involvement in the war. Although searching these files can be very time-consuming, they can provide considerable background information.

Territorial Army

Under the Defence Act of 1909 the Volunteer Corps were reconstituted as the Territorial Army and a system of compulsory military training was set up.

Personnel files are held by Base Records at the Ministry of Defence, Wellington.

New Zealand National Archives hold registers of commissions which includes officers of the Territorial Army.

World War I

Basic details on New Zealand personnel who served in World War I are best obtained from Base Records at the Ministry of Defence but much supplementary material, such as Nominal Embarkation Rolls of the 1st NZEF, is available at the New Zealand National Archives. There are also war diaries of units, divisions, and battalions, Medal Rolls, casualty lists, and active service and casualty forms (except for those who transferred to the Royal Flying Corps), arranged alphabetically. The locations of soldiers' graves and often the next of kin are also recorded.

The National Archives of New Zealand also hold papers from the New Zealand Army Nursing Service. This gives lists of nurses who served in various capacities during World War I, and the Nursing Reserve Lists for 1920 to 1924.

The Army Department holds registers of reservists, arranged in order of ballot and then alphabetically (for full addresses *see* p. 110). There is also an index register of soldiers who resettled between 1916 and 1930.

The 'Turkish War' (the Chanak incident, 1922)

The files of volunteers are located through the Army Departmental series lists.

World War II

The files of individual servicemen and women are held at the Base Records, Ministry of Defence, Wellington.

Other resources

The New Zealand National Archives holds much supplementary material such as the Embarkation Rolls of the second NZEF, war diaries, Medal Rolls, and casualty lists. It also holds cards which give information on the graves of soldiers buried overseas.

For service personnel who served with the Occupation of Japan, the Korean War, the Malaysian Emergency, and Vietnam conflict, all individual files are kept at Base Records, Ministry of Defence, Wellington.

The main material held at the New Zealand National Archives consists of a number of unit war diaries.

Files on conscientious objectors to military service during World War II and later campaigns are restricted.

All the locations of Service Records in New Zealand were extracted from a Draft Copy of a printed guide being prepared by the National Archives Office of New Zealand.

Long Service Medal awarded to H. W. L. Holt, who served with the NSW Volunteer Artillery from 1860 to 1904

PART FIVE

Military memorabilia — old photographs — the Imperial, Australian and New Zealand Uniforms of the 19th century-insignia, buttons and other kit, other military items such as medals — description of campaign medals and ribbons from Waterloo to Vietnam — some Long Service and Good Conduct Medals that were issued during colonial times

Head dress badge of the Queensland Scottish Volunteer Regiment

Memorabilia and medals

Military memorabilia

Items of memorabilia connected with an ancestor's Army service can provide valuable clues. The means of identifying a particular military formation, or being able to pin-point a date, may provide or confirm some missing or doubtful piece of information. It also may be the source of some interesting biographical details.

Family relics such as medals, military insignia, service documents, and old photographs all fall within this category; the most useful relics for providing basic military particulars are military medals. Most of these, especially if they were awarded by the Australian, British or New Zealand governments, will bear the name of the recipient along with rank and corps or regiment. Later issues may include personal or Army number which is useful when researching a fairly common name. Apart from the relics' value as a durable record, many are valuable collectors' items. The rare Peninsular Cross, awarded to officers during the Napoleonic wars, may fetch several thousand (Australian) dollars at an auction. A simple Egypt Medal issued to an Australian soldier in 1885 could be worth at least $A500.

Compared with other European countries Britain was slow to give honours and distinction to its soldiers. Medals to commemorate a particular battle or campaign were sometimes given to senior officers; a junior officer was sometimes rewarded with a gold medal for an act of bravery. This was awarded by his regiment and invariably paid for by his fellow-officers. Officers and soldiers, both British and Indian, who were serving with the Honorable East India Company had been given campaign medals since the conflict in the Deccan in 1784. The Company continued to award medals until its affairs were taken over by the British Government after the Indian Mutiny of 1857 and 1858.

A high proportion of the officers and soldiers who served with the garrisons in Australia or New Zealand would have fought in one or more of the many 19th-century campaigns and wars. These began with the long, hard struggle against the French which ended at Waterloo in 1815. Wars continued throughout many parts of the globe and conflict came slowly to a halt after the South Africa war of 1899 to 1902.

The first of the British Imperial wars involving men from the colonies was fought in the Sudan in 1885. The outrage which followed General Gordon's murder at Khartoum prompted most of the Australian colonies to call for volunteers to aid the British forces in Egypt and the Sudan. This resulted in some 750 volunteer soldiers from New South Wales serving in Egypt and being awarded the British Egypt Medal and the Egyptian Khedive Star. In addition to the official medals, a number of private citizens had medals made for the homecoming troops; the most notable of these was the Mayor of Sydney Silver Medal. Most of the British and old Empire awards for bravery or distinguished service are well documented in official citations, Government *Gazettes*, and the press. Several well-written reference books have been published which deal with the recipients of the Victoria Cross and Distinguished Conduct Medal. Details of the most common campaign medals awarded during the colonial period are listed on page 126-132.

In addition to medals for individual acts of gallantry and participation in a campaign, there were a large number of medals that were given for efficiency, long service, and good conduct. During the reign of William IV (1830-1837) Army authorities adopted a policy of rewarding soldiers for good conduct. These took the form of a badge worn on the jacket, extra pay after seven and fourteen years of crime-free service, and a medal for eighteen-years continuous service. Many years later a similar award was given to members of the militia and volunteer forces. Subsequently members of the locally raised forces in Australia and New Zealand received a corresponding award for either long or efficient service or both.

Before the age of photography any form of portraiture, whether drawn or painted, was too costly for the lower ranks of the military but a number of the more affluent officers have left pictures of them

British Egypt and Sudan Medal with 'Suakin' Clasp and Khedive Star. Awarded in 1885 to Private John Maddison, NSW Infantry

Waterloo Medal awarded to Corporal William Hall, 23rd Light Dragoons, later Royal NSW Veteran Company. (Note the home-made suspender.)

selves. Many of those who became settlers may be seen in private or public collections in Australia and New Zealand.

When attempting to identify military dress in such portraits the family historian is at the mercy of the artist's attention to detail and the ravages of time. Artists with no military experience did not always comprehend the minute variations which occurred in the early 19th-century uniforms. Certain colours were prone to fading and this may cause difficulties when identifying the facing colours which appeared on the collars, cuffs, and turned-back lapels of an Army coat. Insignia and numerals depicted on the wearer's head dress, belt plates or buttons, however, were often shown with remarkable accuracy.

The first photographs to appear were daguerreotypes and these were available in Australia and New Zealand from the late 1840s. This process produced a single, mirror image on a metallic surface which was covered with glass and usually presented in an ornate velvet and leather folder. These photographs required a long exposure time, were small and still relatively expensive. With the invention of the wet-plate collodion process during the early 1850s larger pictures could be printed in unlimited numbers at a lower cost. The process was more suited to outdoor photography.

It was during the early years of wet-plate photography that the volunteer citizen soldier appeared. Very few portraits of the old 1854 Volunteers would have survived and their dark green uniforms with black buttons and the minimum of decoration would not have photo-graphed well. When, in the 1860s, the Volunteer Force became a popular movement, a very large number of pictures were taken. A great variety of uniforms appeared during this period with designs and decorations left to the personal taste of the Commanding Officers. These ranged from the drab grey of the New South Wales Volunteer Infantry to the scarlet coats and plumed helmets worn by the Yeomanry Cavalry. Somewhere between were the Volunteer Artillery with the red-faced blue uniform topped off with a tall, plumed busby.

In New Zealand during the 1860s there was a large force of British troops stationed throughout the North Island and quite a large number of photographs were taken. Those taken in the towns or base camps during the summer usually showed the troops wearing red coats with white trousers. Those taken in winter time usually showed officers in dark blue 'undress' uniforms and the troops in a blue serge patrol jacket and a round forage cap. The latter displayed the number of the regiment in either arabic or roman numerals. The white

Left, *William John Sloan, born Northern Ireland 1831, came to New South Wales at the age of four. He joined the NSW Volunteer Rifle Company in 1860; became Colour Sergeant 1869; Ensign 1870; Major on his retirement. He died in 1916.* Right, *Alexander Wilkinson, born Bathurst 1826, joined NSW Rifle Volunteers 1860; rank of Ensign confirmed 1863; Lieutenant 1866. He died in 1904*

NSW Volunteer Artillery at a training camp, c.1888. BQMS H. W. L. Holt is second from left

trousers were replaced by a dark blue pattern worn with black leather gaiters.

When British soldiers left the South Pacific region in 1870 and small permanent military forces were formed in the various colonies, very few of the members appear to have been photographed. It was when these forces began expanding from the early 1860s that there seems to have been a spate of citizen soldiers presenting themselves to the photographer. In New South Wales there was an upsurge of interest in such activities at the time of the Sudan War in 1885. From this Campaign came the first Australian soldiers to appear in khaki uniforms. By the late 1870s the peaked shako had been replaced in most units by a helmet; these were covered with cloth which varied in colour from blue to buff or white. A plate was generally worn at the front of the helmet which incorporated the coat of arms of the colony. For undress purposes some kind of forage cap was worn which might take the form of the 'pill box', with or without a peak, according to rank, or a form of glengarry. The latter came into favour with both British and colonial troops at a time when Queen Victoria was becoming infatuated with all things Scottish.

By the last decade of the 19th century all colonial armies were acquiring local characteristics and were adopting dress more suited to the local climate and their military qualities. The wide-brimmed felt hat was the choice of many such armies. This form of head dress had formerly been adopted by British and colonial troops serving in the east and west African campaigns and was a variant of the felt hat, turned up at the left-hand side. These were worn by English musketeers in the 17th century, just as the slouch or bush hat was chosen by both colonial and Commonwealth armies of Australia. The exception was the slightly lower crown version, without the turn-up, worn by the Australian Mounted Infantry during the Boer War. A hat similar to this was worn by New Zealand troops. They dented the top of the crown to form what became known as the 'lemon squeezer' hat.

Occasionally items of antique militaria are unearthed which may provide clues to tracking down a forbear. More than a century after British regiments departed from the region, relics are still being found, especially those which had belonged to military settlers. Only rarely is a complete uniform found in a family collection, but smaller articles such as badges, belt plates, and buttons may appear.

Head dress badges are usually quite easy to identify. The regimental number or title is usually displayed as a part of the design. This was usually mounted at the centre of an eight-pointed star which was surmounted by a crown. Variations of this pattern were worn from the 1820s until the close of the 19th century.

The shoulder belt plate covered the buckle which fastened the sword belt of officers and senior NCOs and the cross belt worn by the troops. Originally oval in shape, it became oblong during the Peninsular campaign and was produced in silver gilt for officers and brass for the rank and file. During the 1830s these became more elaborate in design and incorporated regimental or county emblems along with battle honours. Many have become valuable collector's items. Buttons of the Imperial period have occasionally been unearthed and it is not difficult to identify the corps or regiment of the wearer but pinpointing the period needs careful attention. Before 1767 the buttons on British soldiers' coats did not carry a regimental design, but from that year until 1881 the number of the regimental title appeared in some form. This applied to both cavalry and infantry. The most common design was the number displayed within a broken circle with a dot at the opening.

From 1880 the button-makers began to put the name of the manufacturers on the backs of their buttons. The chief firms in this trade were Firmin, Jennens, Nutting, and Smith and Wright. Firmins underwent a number of name changes between 1771 and 1841; Smith and Wright made buttons for the rank and file between 1855 and 1871. The older pewter buttons were made by Messrs Nutting of London; this firm amalgamated with Sherlocks in 1840. The designs of buttons changed little over the years although by the early 19th century many had substituted the circle around the regimental numerals for a wreath of leaves. In the case of some Scottish regiments, such as the 21st, it took the form of thistles. The more convex-shaped larger button issued after 1855 had a closed back and the numeral was sometimes placed on an eight-pointed star. Light Infantry regiments usually included the characteristic Horn and Strings.

In 1871 the Royal Arms replaced all regimental designs on infantry buttons. The regimental pattern button was then only worn by cavalry, artillery, Royal Engineers, Foot Guards, and certain departmental corps. Hussar regiments wore plain ball-shaped buttons.

Several unofficial types of buttons were worn by Army personnel at various times. Those that were worn on officers' black frock coat during the 1840 to 1850 period had the initials of the title of the regiment in a cypher below a crown. There was another type of unofficial button worn on the white coats issued to mess waiters which came into use around 1835. These were usually a flat, single-piece button with the design in relief.

Military service medals awarded to colonial and Imperial troops between 1848 to 1903

Military General Service Medal (MGSM)

Although this medal was awarded for campaigns between 1793 and 1814, it was not issued until 1848. A total of twenty-nine bars were issued for the more important actions and campaigns and some of these commemorated many of the most famous battles in British history.

As veterans of the Peninsular War some early settlers in Australia were recipients of this medal. The bars that were attached to the medals would have included: Barrossa, Busaco, Cuidad Rodrigo

The Waterloo and Military General Service Medals awarded to Private Cooke, 46th Regiment and Royal NSW Veteran Companies.
Above, *the obverse,* below, *the reverse*

Badajoz, Fuentes d'Onor, Albuhera, Salamanca, Talavera, Nivelle, Nive, Pyranees, San Sebastian, Orthes, Toulouse, Vimiera, Roleia. The spelling of these place names will vary.

The ribbon of this medal is crimson with dark blue borders.

Army of India Medal

This medal was issued at the suggestions of the Honorable East India Company and covered campaigns that were fought between 1799 and 1826. It was originally known as the East India Company's General Service Medal and it was not given without a bar. The spelling of the Indian place names on the bars will vary considerably with contemporary spellings.

The colour of the ribbon is light blue.

India General Service Medal

There were three issues of this medal between 1854 and 1903. The 1854 issue was the first to be awarded by the British Government and covered such actions as Pegu, Persia, Bhootan, Burma, Waziristan, Perak, and Sikkim.

The ribbon is crimson with two dark blue stripes.

Indian Mutiny Medal

A number of men who were serving with the 11th (North Devon Regiment and were due for their discharge volunteered to go to India with the Regiment during the Indian Mutiny of 1857 to 1858. A number of veterans of this campaign later settled in either Australia or New Zealand. The bars with this medal include Delhi, Lucknow, and Central India and it was the last medal to be issued by the Honorable East India Company.

The ribbon is white with two ¼ inch scarlet stripes.

Crimea Medal

This was one of the few British war medals that were issued while the war was still in progress, having been authorised in December 1854. A number of ex-soldiers who settled in Australia and New Zealand during the latter half of the 19th century were recipients of this medal. The bars given with it commemorated the battles of Alma, Balaklava, Inkerman, and Sebastopol.

The ribbon is light blue with yellow edges.

Right, *William Hall (1792-1850), formerly a Corporal of the 23rd Light Dragoons and later (1826-29) a Private in the Royal NSW Veteran Company stationed at Newcastle*

Left, *Edward Charles Close (1790-1866) formerly a lieutenant of the 48th (Northamptonshire) Regiment. Close was a founder of the NSW township of Morpeth. This painting, showing him wearing his Military General Service Medal, c.1850, hangs in the Newcastle City Library*

New Zealand Medal 1846-47 and 1860-66 (*see* p. 107)

Egypt 1882-1889 Medal

This was the first British campaign medal to be awarded to colonial as well as imperial troops. This medal was given for the Egyptian War of 1882 and subsequent campaigns in the Sudan which included Suakin which was the first battle honour to be won by a contingent of Australian troops. The bars issued were Tel-el-Kebir, El Teb-Tamai, the Nile, Abu Klea, Kirkeban, Tofrek, and Suakin.

The ribbon is divided into five equal stripes of three bright blue and two white.

The second Indian Service Medal

This medal was issued in 1895 and is sometimes called the India 1895 Medal. A total of ten bars were given with this medal and include such campaigns as Relief of Chitral, Defence of Chitral, Punjab Frontier, Malakand, Samana, and Tirah.

The ribbon for this medal is crimson with two dark blue stripes.

A new India General Service Medal was issued early in the reign of King Edward VII and is similar in design to the 1895 pattern. One bar was given with this medal and this was for Waziristan 1901 and 1902. Very few of these medals were awarded to British personnel.

The ribbon for the 1903 medal is green with a wide central stripe of dark blue.

Campaign medals issued to colonial and Imperial troops between 1816 and 1902

Waterloo Medal

This was issued early in 1816 to all ranks who had fought at Waterloo in June 1815. It established a precedent in the British Army for granting the same medal to officers and rank and file alike.

The ribbon is red with royal blue edges.

Sutlej Medal

This medal was awarded for the Sikh War of 1845 and 1846 and the recipients would have included many officers and soldiers of the 50th and 80th Regiments who had served in the Australian colonies between 1833 and 1845. A number of survivors returned as settlers. The battles fought during this campaign included Aliwal, Moodkee, Ferozeshur, and Sobraon.

The ribbon for this medal is dark blue with crimson edges.

Punjab Medal

Many of the survivors of the previous campaign also took part in the three main battles against the Sikhs which were fought during 1848 and 1849. These were Mooltan, Chilianwala, and Goojerat.

Bars were issued for all three battles.

Khedive Star

This was issued by the Egyptian Government to the British and New South Wales troops who took part in the Egyptian and Sudan campaigns. This medal was not inscribed when issued but many were engraved at the recipient's expense.

The ribbon for this medal is plain dark blue.

Mayor of Sydney's Silver Sudan Medal

This is one of several unofficial medals given to members of the New South Wales contingent when they returned from the Sudan in 1885. This medal was issued uninscribed but many were engraved at the recipient's expense.

The colour of the ribbon varied according to the branch of the service in which the member served. Red for infantry, blue for artillery, and light blue for the ambulance section.

Queen's South Africa Medal

It was one of two medals awarded for service in the Boer War from 1899 to 1902. This medal came with a record number of bars, twenty-six in all.

The ribbon for this medal is red with two blue stripes and a broad orange stripe down the centre.

King's South Africa Medal

This medal was authorised in October 1902 to recognise service in the latter phases of the war in South Africa. More than 16,000 Australian and 6,500 New Zealand soldiers would have received one or both of the South Africa Medals.

Two bars were issued and the colour of the ribbon is green, white and yellow in equal width.

Long Service, Good Conduct and Meritorious Service Medals awarded to colonial and Imperial troops between 1830 and 1903

British soldiers were first awarded medals for Long Service and Good Conduct during the reign of William IV (1830-1837), and subsequently similar awards were made to the auxiliary and colonial forces. It was issued initially with the medal fastened to the ribbon by a steel ring which was replaced during the reign of Queen Victoria by a suspender similar to that on the Indian General Service Medal.

The ribbon was originally plain crimson but was later changed to crimson with a white stripe at each edge.

In 1881 the Volunteer Military Force of the Colony of Victoria commenced issuing a Long and Efficient Service Medal. This was given to all ranks until 1893 when officers were issued with the Volunteer Decoration.

Long Service and Meritorious Service Medals were awarded by the Colonial Military Forces, with the exception of Western Australia, between 1894 and 1903. Very few of these medals were issued and, although the Commonwealth of Australia was established in 1901, awards of these medals continued until 1903.

Campaign Medals of World War I, 1914 to 1918

1914 Star

The first medal to be awarded for World War I is often incorrectly referred to as the Mons Star. The medal has the words 'Aug.' and 'Nov.' above and below 1914 respectively.

The ribbon is red white and blue, shaded and watered.

1914-15 Star

The same design and ribbon as above, but the words 'Aug.' and 'Nov.' are omitted and the dates 1914-15 appears in place of 1914.

Victory Medal

This is a poor quality medal but more than 5,000,000 were issued. It is made of bronze and the reverse side bears the inscription: 'The Great War for Civilisation'.

The ribbon is a watered rainbow pattern; recipients who were mentioned in dispatches wear the bronze oak leaf on the ribbon.

The British War Medal

Although more than 5.5 million were issued, this medal is made of silver and is of some intrinsic value. The reverse side shows the figure of St George on horseback.

The ribbon has a broad orange stripe bordered with white, black, and blue stripes.

Territorial Force War Medal

This medal was given to men who had served in the Territorial Force which, in the United Kingdom, had replaced the old Volunteer Force in 1907. The reverse side bears the inscription 'For Voluntary Service Overseas'.

The ribbon is watered yellow with two green stripes.

World War II, Korean War and minor campaigns

For the numerous campaigns which made up World War II, the British Government issued eight stars and two medals. The Australian and New Zealand Governments issued one medal each.

1939-45 Star

This star was first authorised in 1943 as the 1943 Star but was only issued as a ribbon to those who had taken part in early campaigns such as Norway, France, and Belgium in 1940.

The ribbon is dark blue, red and light blue in equal stripes. A bar was given to Air Force personnel who took part in the Battle of Britain.

Atlantic Star

This star was issued mainly to naval personnel but was also given to Air Crew who had taken part in operations over the Atlantic.

The ribbon is dark blue, white and sea green, shaded and watered. Bars were given for those who were also entitled to the France and Germany Star and the Air Crew Europe Star.

Air Crew Europe Star

Awarded to Air Force personnel with operational service over Europe. Bars were given to those who were entitled to the Atlantic and France and Germany Stars.

The ribbon is light blue with black edges and two yellow stripes.

Africa Star

Awarded to all services that had taken part in campaigns in North Africa between 1940 and 1943. The figures '1' and '8' stitched on the ribbon denotes that the recipient served with the First or Eighth Armies.

The ribbon is pale buff, central red stripe and one dark blue and one light blue stripe.

Pacific Star

This medal was awarded to Australian and British forces that had taken part in campaigns in the Pacific and South-East Asia regions. A bar was given to those who were entitled to the Burma Star.

The ribbon is dark green with red edges, a yellow central stripe and a thin dark blue and a thin light blue stripe.

Burma Star

This medal was awarded mainly to British forces that had served in campaigns fought to the east of Calcutta between 1941 and 1945. A bar was given to those who were entitled to the Pacific Star.

The ribbon is dark blue with a wide red central stripe and two orange stripes.

Italy Star

This medal was awarded to all British Commonwealth forces that took part in actions fought in Italy and Yugoslavia between 1943 and 1945 A large number of Australian Air Force and New Zealand Army personnel would be entitled to this Star.

The ribbon is equal stripes of red, white, green, white, and red.

France and Germany Star

Awarded to those taking part in the battles which followed the 'D Day' landings up until the armistice of May 1945. Bars were given to Air Force personnel who were entitled to the Atlantic and Air Crew Europe stars.

The ribbon is blue, white, red, and blue in equal stripes.

Defence Medal

This medal was awarded to members of the Armed Forces and auxiliary services that had served in Britain during the air raids or had served in a danger area for one year overseas.

The ribbon is flame-coloured, green edges with two thin black stripes.

British War Medal 1939-45

This medal was awarded for at least twenty-eight days' service in the Navy, Army or Air Force between 3 September 1939 and May 1945.

The ribbon has a central narrow red stripe on a white stripe on a wide dark blue stripe and edged with red.

Unfortunately the majority of British medals and stars awarded for service in World War II were not issued with the receipients' names although some were engraved privately.

Australian War Medal

The obverse side of this medal bears the Australian Coat of Arms and is inscribed 'Australian Service Medal 1939-1945'.

The ribbon is a wide central stripe of light grey between two narrow red stripes with the edges banded with light blue on the left and dark blue on the right.

New Zealand War Medal

This medal has an unusual suspender which takes the form of two fern leaves; it is inscribed 'For Service to New Zealand 1939-1945'.

The ribbon is dark grey, edged with white stripes.

British Korea Medal

This medal was awarded to all British and Commonwealth forces that served in the Korean War from July 1951.

The ribbon is yellow with two blue stripes.

United Nations Korea Medal

This medal was issued to all Allied forces that served during the Korean War. It is bronze and the obverse side bears the insignia of the United Nations.

The ribbon is white with nine narrow blue stripes.

General Service Medal

This medal has been awarded to British and Commonwealth forces for campaign service in many parts of the world. These date from the South Persia expedition in 1918 through to the emergencies in Malaya and the disturbances in Cyprus and Northern Ireland. The obverse side of the medal bears the inscription 'For Campaign Service' below a crown.

The ribbon is purple with a broad green central stripe.

Regimental medals

Compared with other countries Britain was never lavish in awarding medals to its soldiers until the Military General Service Medal (MGSM) was issued in 1849. Before then it was customary for regiments to give medals to officers and rank and file for either deeds of gallantry or to commemorate a particular battle. The cost of manufacturing these was borne by the officers.

Following the award of the Waterloo Medal in 1816, many veterans who had fought long and hard during the Peninsular Campaign were to receive nothing until the issue of the MGSM more than thirty years later. In an attempt to fill this gap some medals were awarded by at least two regiments (the 48th and 88th) to their men who had fought in various battles of the Peninsular War. When the 48th (Northamptonshire) Regiment arrived in Australia in 1817 almost half of its members had served in this Campaign. While the Regiment was stationed in Australia a number of these medals were awarded.

According to the research that was carried out by T. C. Sargent of the Military Historical Society of Australia, at least twenty-five of these veterans are known to have settled in New South Wales or Tasmania. The medals that were issued during the Regiment's stay were, according to Mr L. Carlisle and Major P. Boland, made by Sydney engraver Samuel Clayton. The ribbon is Waterloo Medal ribbon and would have been ordered from England.

Back badge of a soldier of the 28th (North Gloucester) Regiment. A unique distinction worn at the back of the head dress to commemorate a 'back to back' engagement with the French in 1801

Head dress badge of the 4th NSW Volunteer Infantry

Indian General Service Medal (1854) with 'Pegu' Clasp

Head dress badge of the Volunteer Infantry of Victoria

Locations of Medal Records

United Kingdom
The award of campaign medals from 1793 to 1912 is recorded on rolls which are kept at the Public Record Office, Kew, under WO 100. These are available on microfilm in the Reading Room on open access. Records of campaign medals from World War I onwards are kept at The Army Medal Office, Government Buildings, Droithwich, Worcestershire, WR9 8AU, England.

Australia
Inquiries regarding Australian medals should be addressed to Department of Defence, Russell Office, Canberra, ACT 2600.

New Zealand
Medal Rolls for awards of the Queen's South Africa Medal and the King's South Africa Medal are held at the New Zealand National Archives Office. Other Medal Rolls are kept at the Army Department Archives at Base Records, Ministry of Defence, Wellington, New Zealand.

Glossary of military terms and abbreviations

ADC	Aide-de-camp. Usually an officer assisting a General
Adjutant	An appointment, not a rank. An officer who assists the Commanding Officer
AHC	Army Hospital Corps, formed in 1856
AJCP	Australian Joint Copying Project
Attestation	The formal swearing-in of a recruit
bearskin	A tall fur head dress formerly worn by Grenadier Company, Drum-Majors and sometimes Band-Masters. They are still worn by the Brigade of Guards in full dress
BNI	Bengal Native Infantry
Bombardier	A junior Non-Commissioned Officer of artillery
Brevet rank	An unpaid, honourary rank
BSM	Battery Sergeant-Major
busby	A fur cap, smaller than the bearskin, worn by Artillery and Hussars
CB	Companion of the Order of the Bath
CB	Confined to barracks. A minor punishment
CIE	Companion of the Order of the Indian Empire
Chelsea Pensioner	Formerly an ex-soldier who is receiving a long service or disability pension. At the present time it is a pensioned soldier who is in the care of the Royal Hospital, Chelsea
Cmdt	Commandant

Commissariat	The department which was responsible for supplying the Army with food
CO	Commanding Officer
Cornet	The most junior commissioned rank in the cavalry
Cpl	Corporal
CSC	Commissariat Staff Corps
DAG	Deputy Adjutant-General
DCM	Distinguished Conduct Medal
DIH	Deputy Inspector of Hospitals
Dmr	Drummer
ED	Efficiency Decoration
EM	Efficiency Medal
Ensign	The most junior commissioned rank in the infantry. It was replaced by a rank of 2nd Lieutenant
Espontoon	A pole weapon carried by officers during the 18th century
Facings	The colours worn on cuffs and collars to denote regiment
Fencible	A member of a regiment raised for home service only
FM	Field Marshal
Furlough	Leave of absence
Fusilier	A soldier who was formerly trained to defend the Artillery
GCMG	Knight Grand Cross of the Order of St Michael & St George
GHQ	General Headquarters
GOC	General Officer Commanding
Gorget	A small, crescent-shaped plate worn by officers at the front of their collars to denote that they were on duty. Gorgets were abolished in 1830
Grenadiers	A soldier trained to throw grenades and formed into companies before 1862. They were usually the tallest men in the regiment
Halberd	A pole weapon carried by sergeants before 1812
HBM	His/Her Britannic Majesty
HEIC	Honorable East India Company
HG	Horse Guards. The title formerly given to the War Office

i/c	In charge of
IDC	Passed Imperial Defence College
IMS	Indian Medical Service
ISO	Imperial Service Order
JAG	Judge-Advocate General
Jemadar	A junior commissioned officer, Indian Army
KB	Knight Bachelor
KBE	Knight of the Order of the British Empire
KCIE	Knight Commander of the Order of the Indian Empire
KCVO	Knight Commander of the Victorian Order
KR	King's Regulations
KH	Knight of the Guelphic Hanoverian Order, abolished 1837
Lance rank	A soldier who is appointed to act as the next rank senior to the one he is holding
LG	Life Guards
Lieut.	Lieutenant
Light Company	A flank company trained in scouting and skirmishing. The company was abolished in 1862
Maj.	Major
MBE	Member of the Order of the British Empire
MC	Military Cross. Instituted for officers in 1914
MM	Military Medal. Instituted for Non-Commissioned Officers and Privates in 1916
MO	Medical Office
MVO	Member of the Victorian Order
Naik	Junior non-commissioned officer, Indian Army
NCO	Non-commissioned officer
NZEF	New Zealand Expeditionary Force
OBE	Officer of the Order of the British Empire
OC	Officer commanding
OR	Other rank. The rank and file
OTC	Officer's Training Corps
PMG	Paymaster General
psa	Passed Staff College, Andover
psc	Passed Staff College, Camberley
Pte or Pvt	A private soldier
QM	Quartermaster
QMG	Quartermaster-General

QMS	Quartermaster-Sergeant
RA	Royal Artillery
RE	Royal Engineers
Regt	Regiment
RHG	Royal Horse Guards
RMA	Royal Military Academy
RMLI	Royal Marine Light Infantry
R of O	Reserve of Officers
SEATO	South-East Asia Treaty Organisation
Sergt or Sgt	Sergeant
Shako	A peaked head dress worn by soldiers during the 19th century
SM	Sergeant-Major
Stock	A neck band worn under the collar. Velvet for officers and thin leather for the rank and file, abolished in 1855
Subahdar	Junior commissioned rank, Indian Army
TA	Territorial Army, Britain and New Zealand
TD	Territorial Decoration
Tpr	Trooper
Tptr	Trumpeter
VC	Victoria Cross, instituted 1856
VCO	Viceroy Commissioned Office, Indian Army
VD	Volunteer Decoration
VD	Venereal Disease
Volunteer (1)	A part-time, usually unpaid, soldier
Volunteer (2)	An applicant for a commissioned rank who cannot afford to purchase but serves without pay until a vacancy occurs.
WD	War Department
WO	Warrant-Officer
Yeomanry	Cavalry in the Volunteer Force

Appendices

Appendix 1   A quick guide to the Public Record Office volume or piece numbers and microfilm numbers of the Royal Artillery in Australia and New Zealand

Unit	Tour of duty	WO 10 volume or piece numbers	AJCP reel numbers
2nd Company	Aug. 1845 to	1940, 1967,	6019
6th Battalion	Sept. 1856	1997, 2000,	6019
		2025, 2026/1	6019
		2049/2, 2050,	6019
		2076, 2077,	6020
		2099, 2109,	6020
		2139, 2140,	6020
		2173, 2174,	6020 and 6021
		2197, 2212,	6021
		2213, 2250,	6021
		2251	6021
8th Company	Apr. 1856 to	2276, 2289,	6021, 6022
10th Battalion	Sept. 1858	2307, 2322	6022
1st Battery	Aug. 1868 to	2392, 2393,	6022
1st Brigade	Jun. 1870	2394, 2395,	6022
		2396, 2397,	6022
		2398, 2399	6022 and 6023

Appendix 2   A quick guide to microfilm numbers of British Infantry Regiments in Australia and New Zealand with the Public Record Office volume/piece number and the AJCP reel numbers

3rd	Aust.	Dec. 1822-Dec. 1827	2118-2119	3694-3696
4th	Aust.	Jan. 1831-Mar. 1838	2213-2219	3696-3699
11th	Aust.	Apr. 1845-Mar. 1858	2874-2890	3703-3714
12th	Aust. & NZ	Apr. 1858-Aug. 1868	2971-2994	3714-3732
14th				
2nd Battn.	Aust. & NZ	Apr. 1860-Dec. 1870	3206-3219	3734-3748
17th	Aust.	Dec. 1828-Mar. 1836	3434-3438	3748-3750
18th				
2nd Battn.	Aust. & NZ	Apr. 1863-Mar. 1870	3578-3585	3750-3758
21st	Aust.	Apr. 1832-Mar. 1841	3802-3809	3758-3763
28th	Aust.	Apr. 1835-Mar. 1843	4443-4450	3764-3768
39th	Aust.	Dec. 1824-Mar. 1833	5263-5266	3770-3772
40th	Aust.	Dec. 1823-Dec. 1828	5336-5339	3772-3774
40th	Aust. & NZ	Apr. 1852-Sept. 1856	5363-5386	3774-3792
43rd	NZ	Apr. 1863-Mar. 1866	5618-5620	3792-3795
46th	Aust.	Dec. 1812-Dec. 1817	5809-5810	3795-3796
48th	Aust.	Dec. 1815-Dec. 1824	5969-5974	3796-3799
50th	Aust.	Apr. 1834-Mar. 1842	6127-6134	3799-3802
50th	Aust. & NZ	Apr. 1863-Mar. 1869	6156-6162	3802-3809
51st	Aust.	Apr. 1837-Mar. 1847	6200-6209	3809-3815
57th	Aust.	Dec. 1824-Mar. 1833	6650-6656	3816-3818
57th	NZ	Apr. 1860-Jul. 1867	6683-6695	3818-3826
58th	Aust. & NZ	Apr. 1843-Mar. 1859	6743-6761	3826-3837
63rd	Aust.	Dec. 1827-Mar. 1834	7261-7265	3839-3841
65th	Aust. & NZ	Apr. 1845-Dec. 1865	7415-7446	3841-3860
68th	NZ	Apr. 1863-Mar. 1866	7676-7678	3860-3862
70th	NZ	Feb. 1861-Dec. 1865	7830-7835	3863-3868
73rd	Aust.	Dec. 1808-Dec. 1815	8000-8002	3868-3870
77th	Aust.	Apr. 1857-Mar. 1859	8293-8294	3875-3877
80th	Aust.	Apr. 1836-Mar. 1845	8478-8486	3880-3884
96th	Aust. & NZ	Apr. 1839-Mar. 1849	9611-9623	3889-3896
99th	Aust. & NZ	Apr. 1841-Mar. 1857	9804-9822	3896-3905
NSW Corps		June 1789-Dec. 1797	11028	417
102nd	Aust.	Jul. 1798-Dec. 1812	9399-9905	412-416
				3906-3910

First Fleet Marines

These records were kept by the Admiralty and have been recently microfilmed by the Australian Joint Copying Project. The reel number is 412 but it includes very little biographical information about the individual Marines

Appendix 3   British support troops in Australia and New Zealand

Veteran Company NSW	Australia	March 1810 to September 1823	1128 to 1129	417 to 419
Royal NSW Veteran Company	Australia	June 1826 to June 1832	11230	3917
Royal Staff Corps	Australia	September 1826 to October 1829	11084 to 11087	3917
Commissariat Staff Corps	NZ	May 1861 to July 1868	10655 to 10670	3913 to 3914
Commissariat Transport Corps	NZ	July 1861 to June 1866	10678 to 10681	3914 to 3916
4th Military Train and Horse Transport	NZ	April 1865 to October 1867	10977 to 11008	3916 to 3917
Army Hospital Corps	NZ	March 1861 to October 1870	10432 to 10448	3910 to 3911

Appendix 4   Useful addresses, military records

England: The Keeper
Public Record Office
Ruskin Avenue, Kew
Richmond, Surrey TW9 4DU UK

Army Medal Office
Government Building
Droitwich
Worcestershire, WR9 8AU

The Library
India Office
197 Blackfriars Road
London SE1 8NG UK

The Library
National Army Museum
Royal Hospital Road
Chelsea SW3 4HT UK

Royal Marine Barracks
Southsea
Hampshire UK

Ireland:	Military Historical Society of Ireland
	1 Northgate Street
	Athlone
	County Meath Ireland
Australia:	Information Support Group
	Central Army Records Office
	PO Box 1932R
	Melbourne 3001

Australian War Memorial
PO Box 34
Dickson 2601

Victoria Barracks Museum
Paddington 2021

New Zealand: Assistance Chief, Defence Staff
Personnel Branch, Defence HQ
Private Bag, Wellington NZ

The Curator
Auckland Institute and Museum
Private Bag, Auckland NZ

The Director
New Zealand National Archives Office
129-141 Vivian Street
Wellington NZ

The Curator
Queen Elizabeth Memorial Museum
Waioura
Kings County NZ

New Zealand National Archives (Auckland Branch)
Cnr Hardinge and Graham Streets
Auckland NZ

Officer-in-Charge
Archives Department
New Zealand Police Department
Wellington NZ

Taranaki Museum
PO Box 315
New Plymouth NZ

Bibliography

Atkinson, C. T. *The 39th and 54th Foot* Oxford: Oxford University Press 1947.

Barton, L. L. *Australia and the Waikato War* Sydney: L.A.H. 1979.

—— *The 43rd Light Infantry in New Zealand* Sydney: L.A.H. 1979.

Baxter, A. *Tracing Your Origins* Sydney: Methuen-Australia 1983.

Becket, I. F. L. *Victoria's Wars* Aylesbury: Shire Publishing 1974.

Blaxland, G. *The Buffs* Reading: Osprey Publishing, UK, 1972.

Blumberg, H. E. *Britain's Sea Soldiers* Devenport: Swiss and Co. 1927.

Bowling, A. W. *British Infantry Regiments* London: Almark 1974.

Burge, L. *NSW Military Land Grants* Sydney: NSW Military History Society 1976.

Cannon, R. *Historical Records of the 73rd* Parker, Furnival & Parker 1851.

—— *Historical Records of the 12th* Parker, Furnival & Parker 1848.

—— *Historical Records of the 46th* Parker, Furnival & Parker 1851

Coleman, K. *A Short History of the Military Forces in New South Wales 1770-1900* Sydney: Victoria Barracks Museum Society, 1977.

Connolly, T. W. J. *History of the Royal Engineers* London: Longman, Brown & Green 1855.

Corbett, D. A. *Regimental Badges of New Zealand* Auckland: R. Richards 1986.

Cooper, L. I. *The King's Own* Oxford: Oxford University Press 1939.

Cresswell, J. *Collecting Coins & Medals* Christchurch: Whitcomb & Tombs 1973.

Easty, J. *Voyage to Botany Bay* etc, Sydney: Angus & Robertson 1965.

Fraser, A. *Cromwell Our Chief of Men* London: Weidenfield & Nicolson 1973.

Gibson, T. *The Wiltshire Regiment (62nd & 99th Foot)* London: Leo Cooper 1969.

Gretton, Le G. *Campaigns & History of the Royal Irish* Edinburgh: Blackwood 1911.

Gurney, R. *History of the Northamptonshires* Aldershot: Gale & Polden 1935.

Haydon, A. L. *The Trooper Police of Australia* London: Melrose 1911.

Kipling & King *Head Dress Badges of the British Army* London: Muller 1978.

Laffin, J. *British Campaign Medals* London: Abelard & Schuman 1964.

Money-Barnes, R. *Regiments & Uniforms of the British Army* London: Sphere Books 1972.

Mostyn, E. *Clarks in Australia* Kempsey: Pri. Published 1986.

Mowle, L. M. *Genealogical History of Pioneer Families* Adelaide: Rigby, 1978.

Parkyn, H. G. *Shoulder Belt Plates and Buttons etc* Gale & Polden 1956.

Serle, P. *Dictionary of Australian Biography* Sydney: Angus & Robertson 1949.

Sexton, R. *The Deserters* Magill: Australian Maritime Historical Society 1984.

Taylor, M. (ed.) *The Journal of Ensign Best* Auckland: New Zealand Government Printer 1966.

Wedd, M. *Australian Military Uniforms* Sydney: Kenthurst Kangaroo 1982.

Williams, R. D. *Medals to Australia* 1st edn, Malvern: Skinner & Warnes 1981, 2nd edn, Malvern: Rennicks Books 1983.

Journals, newspapers and standard works of reference

Australian 17 March 1829.

Dollery E. M. 'Military History of Tasmania'. *Journal of the Royal Society of Tasmania.*

Historical Records of Australia series 1, vols 1 XV series 3, vol. 1 (Tasmania).

Journal of Army Historical Research vol. XXXVIII (1960).

Parliamentary Papers 1847, pp. 611-14.

Passmore J. 'The Royal Staff Corps' *Descent* vol. VII, part 1 (1974).

Public Record Office, London. Records of Officers and Soldiers, etc; AJCP Handbook No. 4, War Office.

Returns of the Colony (NSW) 'Blue Books' 1823-1851.

Sydney Gazette 8 September 1823; 12 June 1826; 16 September 1826.

Sabretache vol. xxvii, No. 1, 1987.

Sargent, T. C. 'The First Medal to Troops in Australia'.

White, A. S. 'Garrison, Reserve and Veteran Companies' *Journal of Army Historical Research.*

Index

Norfolk Island 12, 14, 16, 59, 62, 63, 67
North America 16, 45, 51, 82

O'Connell, Lieutenant-General Sir Maurice Charles 45, 68
Ohaiani Pah 70
Orakau 102
Oriental Queen 105
Otago 106
Otahuhu 100

Pacific Star 134
Panmunjom 110
Parihaka
Parliament, British 19, 21, 25
Parramatta 15, 16, 60, 61, 66, 68, 81
Peninsula Campaign 47, 49, 51, 53, 65, 67, 126, 136
Pensions, Pensioners 28-29, 32-34, 39
permanent forces 17
Permanent Militia, New Zealand 97, 113
Phillip, Governor Arthur 12
Phoenix 52
photographs 120, 122
Plymouth 41
police, civilian 14, 15, 67, 107
  see also Mounted Police
Poona 66
Porpoise, HMS 43
Port Dalrymple *see* Launceston
Port Essington 41, 42
Port Phillip district 15, 61, 62
Portsmouth 41
Poverty Bay 99
Preston, Captain H. E. W. 101
Prestonjee Bomanjee 72

Punjab Medal 131
Putahi Pah 62

Quartermaster-General's Department 54
Queensland 17
Queen's South Africa Medal 131

Raby Castle 73
Ramilllies 70, 105
Rangariri 74
Rangiaohia 102
'rank and file' 29
regiments
  naming of 20-21
  origin of in British Army 19
  strength of 19-20
  Devonshire 71
  Dorsetshire 59
  East Surrey 102
  Gloucester 26
  Gloucestershire 66
  King's Own Yorkshire 68
  Manchester 60, 69
  Middlesex 53, 73
  Oxfordshire and Buckinghamshire 100
  Prince of Wales' Own West Yorkshire 74
  South Lancashire 53
  South Staffordshire 67
  West Kent 62
  Wiltshire 70
  3rd 40, 49, 51-52, 53
  4th 40, 61
  11th 40, 70-71
  12th 17, 40, 72-73, 96
  14th 14, 15, 40, 74, 96
  17th 15, 40, 60
  18th 40, 75-77, 96
  21st 40, 62-63

Singapore 86, 110
Sir George Seymour 105
Sir Godfrey Webster 49
Sir Robert Sale 105
Sloan, Major William John 123
Smith and Wright 126
Somersetshire 69
South African War *see* Boer War
Sri Lanka *see* Ceylon
Staffordshire 46
Stewart, Lieutenant-Colonel
    William 51
Stokes Pah 68
Suakin 18, 84, 130
Sudan, Sudan War 17-18, 84, 88,
    92, 120, 124, 130, 131
Sutlej Medal 130-131
Swan River 59, 62, 68
Sydney 15, 16, 43, 47, 53, 59, 61,
    64, 67, 68, 69, 70, 71, 73, 74,
    76, 81, 84
Sydney Gazette 45

Tamar River 41, 58
Taranaki, Taranaki campaign
    73, 99, 100, 106
Tasmania 15, 70, 84, 106, 136
    (*see also* Van Diemen's Land)
Tauranga 99, 102
Te Hoku Whitu Atu 111
Te Kooti 99
Te Papa 102
Te Ranga 100, 102
Territorial Army (Force) 18, 114
Territorial Force War Medal 133
Thompson, Corporal James 107
Times of London 21
Torres Straits 62
Torres Straits Islanders
    see Aborigines

training 20
    compulsory 18, 87
'Turkish War' *see* Chanak
    incident

uniform 122, 124
United Nations 87, 91
United Nations Korea Medal
    136
United States of America 52
'unlimited service' 14

Van Diemen's Land 15, 39, 41,
    49, 52, 54, 55, 58, 59, 60, 62,
    63, 68, 69
Victoria 15, 17, 52, 61, 82, 106,
    132
Victoria Barracks 62
Victory Medal 133
Vietnam, Vietnam War 19, 92,
    94, 111, 115
Volunteer Corps, New Zealand
    97, 113
Volunteer Infantry of Victoria
    137
Volunteers 17, 81-82, 122
Vladivostok 16, 82

Waiari 102
Waikato 74, 99, 102, 106
Waikato Militia 106, 107
Waitangi, Treaty of 14, 67, 100
Wanganui 53, 71, 104
War Office 22, 25, 27, 49, 54, 63
War Office Act, 1870 22, 25
Waterloo, Battle of 47, 52, 65,
    67, 69, 120, 130
Waterloo Medal 130, 136
Wellington 106, 107
Western Australia 39, 59, 68, 69,
    82, 84, 132